STERLING
Test Prep

Law Essentials

Trusts and Estates

Governing Law

3rd edition

Copyright © 2022 Sterling Test Prep

All rights reserved. This publication's content, including the text and graphic images or part thereof, may not be reproduced, downloaded, disseminated, published, converted to electronic media, or distributed by any means whatsoever without prior written consent from the publisher. Copyright infringement violates federal law and is subject to criminal and civil penalties.

This publication is designed to provide accurate and authoritative information regarding the subject matter covered. It is distributed with the understanding that the publisher, authors, or editors are not engaged in rendering legal or another professional service. If legal advice or other expert assistance is required, a competent professional's services should be sought.

Sterling Test Prep is not legally liable for mistakes, omissions, or inaccuracies in this publication's content. Sterling Test Prep does not guarantee that the user of this publication will pass the bar exam or achieve a performance level. Individual performance depends on many factors, including but not limited to the level of preparation, aptitude, and individual performance on test day.

3 2 1

ISBN-13: 978-1-9547252-3-2

Sterling Test Prep products are available at quantity discounts.

For more information, contact info@sterling–prep.com.

Sterling Test Prep
6 Liberty Square #11
Boston, MA 02109

©2022 Sterling Test Prep

Published by Sterling Test Prep

Printed in the U.S.A.

Customer Satisfaction Guarantee

Your feedback is important because we strive to provide the highest quality prep materials. Email us comments or suggestions.

info@sterling–prep.com

We reply to emails – check your spam folder

Thank you for choosing our book!

STERLING
Test Prep

Thousands of students use our study aids to prepare for law school exams and to pass the bar!

Passing the bar is essential for admission to practice law and launching your legal career.

This preparation guide describes the principles of substantive law governing the correct answers to exam questions. It was developed by legal professionals and law instructors who possess extensive credentials and have been admitted to practice law in several jurisdictions. The content is clearly presented and systematically organized for targeted preparation.

The performance on individual questions has been correlated with success or failure on the bar. By analyzing previously administered exams, the authors identified these predictive items and assembled the rules of law that govern the answers to questions tested. Learn the essential governing law to make fine-line distinctions among related principles and decide between tough choices on the exam. This knowledge is vital to excel in law school finals and pass the bar exam.

We look forward to being an essential part of your preparation and wish you great success in the legal profession!

Law Essentials series

Constitutional Law

Contracts

Evidence

Real Property

Torts

Civil Procedure

Criminal Law and Criminal Procedure

Business Associations

Conflict of Laws

Family Law

Secured Transactions

Trusts and Estates

Visit our Amazon store

Comprehensive Glossary of Legal Terms

Over 2,100 essential legal terms defined and explained. An excellent reference source for law students, practitioners and readers seeking an understanding of legal vocabulary and its application.

Landmark U.S. Supreme Court Cases: Essential Summaries

Learn important constitutional cases that shaped American law. Understand how the evolving needs of society intersect with the U.S. Constitution. Short summaries of seminal Supreme Court cases focused on issues and holdings.

Visit our Amazon store

Table of Contents

TRUSTS AND ESTATES GOVERNING LAW 17

    The Probate Estate 19
        Distribution of the estate 19
        Partnership property 19
        Property held in a fiduciary capacity 19
        Jointly-held property 19
        Completed gifts 19
        Causes of action – survival 20
        Causes of action – wrongful death actions 20
        Life insurance and rights under pension plans 20

    Intestate Distribution of Estate 21
        Complete and partial intestacy 21
        Statutory disposition 21
        Spouse survives 21
        Spouse and issue survive 22
        Spouse and kindred survive 22
        Spouse survives, but no issue or kindred survive 22
        Issue survive 22
        No issue survive, but parents survive 22
        No issue and no parents survive, but siblings or their issue survive 23
        No issue, parents, siblings, or their issue survive 23
        Escheat 23
        Additional rules of intestate distribution 24
        Half-blood 24
        Children born out of wedlock 24
        Posthumous children 25
        Limitation of rights of heir or legatee who kills testator 25

    Execution of Wills 27
        Contract to make a will 27
        Age for capacity to execute a will 27
        Testamentary capacity 27
        Testamentary intent 28
        Written requirements for the execution of a valid will 28
        Signature required by the testator or at their express direction 28
        Proper attestation 29
        Interested witnesses 29
        Codicils 30

TRUSTS AND ESTATES GOVERNING LAW (*continued*)

Revocation and Revival of Wills ... 31
- Will revocation ... 31
- Revocation by an instrument executed in the same manner ... 31
- Revocation by intentional destruction ... 31
- Conditional or dependent relative revocation ... 32
- Revival of revoked wills ... 32

Special Circumstances Affecting Intestate and Testate Distribution ... 33
- Simultaneous death ... 33
- Advancement ... 34
- Renunciation of property interests ... 34
- Limitations on testamentary dispositions ... 34
- Spouse's elective share ... 34
- If issue survive ... 35
- If kin survive, but no issue survive ... 35
- If no issue or kin survive ... 35
- Children not mentioned in the will (pretermitted children) ... 36
- No limitations on charitable bequests ... 37
- Provisions in restraint of marriage ... 37

Interpretation and Construction of Wills ... 39
- Incorporation by reference ... 39
- Facts of independent significance ... 39
- Alterations and interlineations ... 39
- Ambiguities ... 40
- Patent ambiguities ... 40
- Latent ambiguities ... 40

Construction of Terms for Relationship and Survivorship ... 41
- Heirs and next of kin ... 41
- Then living ... 41
- Adopted children ... 41
- Construction of devises ... 41
- Exercise of a general power of appointment ... 41

Changes in Property, Beneficiaries and Marital Status Before Death ... 43
- Classification of testamentary dispositions ... 43
- Effect of change in assets between execution and death ... 43
- Specific bequests – ademption by extinction ... 43
- Pecuniary bequests – ademption by satisfaction ... 44

TRUSTS AND ESTATES GOVERNING LAW (continued)

Changes in Property, Beneficiaries and Marital Status Before Death (continued)

Changes in securities	44
Encumbered property	44
Lapse – changes in beneficiaries	44
The anti-lapse statute	44
Class gifts – definition of a class	45
Time to determine membership	45
Changes in marital status – marriage	46
Changes in marital status – divorce	46
Community property	46

The Distribution of the Estate After Death — 49

The estate at the time of death	49
Will contests	49
Improper execution	50
Lack of testamentary capacity	50
Undue influence	50
Fraud in the inducement	50
Fraud in the *factum*	51
Remedies for fraud and undue influence	51
Other reasons for the invalidity of a will	52
Issues altering the operation of the will	52
Collection of the assets of the estate	52
Debts owed by the executor to the estate	52
Income from specifically bequeathed assets	52
Real estate – heirs or devisees normally have control	52
Executor may sell real estate to pay debts and expenses	53
Powers and duties of a fiduciary	53
Standard of executor's obligations	53
Liability of executor or administrator	53
Payment of debts and claims	53
Priority of secured debts with collateral	54
Suits for services – claimant can testify	54
Claim to leave property by will	54
Debts due to the executor	55
Note of claim filed against an estate	55
Disallowance of claims	55
Payments during the statutory period	55
Statute of limitations for suits against the estate	55

TRUSTS AND ESTATES GOVERNING LAW (*continued*)

Exceptions to Statute of Limitations for Suits Against the Estate ... 57
- New assets in an estate ... 57
- Claim not yet accrued ... 57
- Claim satisfied out of insurance ... 57
- Tax returns ... 57

Payment of Legacies and Distributive Shares ... 59
- Payment to spouse in intestacy without issue ... 59
- Time of the payment of legacies ... 59
- Legacies to executor, debtors, and creditors ... 59
- Abatement of legacies ... 60

Completion of the Administration of the Estate ... 61
- Filing account ... 61
- Challenge to account ... 61
- Finality of account ... 61

Conflict of Laws for Wills ... 63
- Domicile ... 63
- Choice of law application ... 64

Definition of a Trust ... 65
- Trusts divide legal and equitable interests ... 65
- Distinguished from other relationships ... 65
- Agency ... 65
- Debtor–creditor ... 65
- Bailment ... 65

Voluntarily Created Trusts ... 67
- Methods of trust creation ... 67
- Trust creation by declaration ... 67
- Trust creation by transfer ... 67
- Voluntary or donative trusts ... 67
- Trusts created by contract ... 68
- Testamentary or *inter vivos* trusts ... 68
- Pour-over provisions for testamentary trusts ... 68
- Savings account trust ... 69
- Gifts to minors ... 69

TRUSTS AND ESTATES GOVERNING LAW (continued)

Required Elements of a Trust 71
- Capacity of the settlor 71
- Necessity for writing 71
- Trust property 72
- Definite or ascertainable beneficiaries 72
- Valid trust purpose 72
- Time restrictions 72

Defining Characteristics of Charitable Trusts 73
- Charitable purpose 73
- Indefinite class of beneficiaries 73
- Similarities to private trusts 73

Limitations of Private Trusts Inapplicable to Charitable Trusts 75
- Rule against perpetuities inapplicable 75
- Failure of purpose 75
- Enforcing the trust 75

Spendthrift Provisions 77
- Protections for beneficiaries 77

Administration of the Trust by the Trustee 79
- Appointment of the trustee 79
- Resignation or removal of the trustee 79
- Compensation of the trustee 79

Powers of the Trustee 81
- Power of sale or contract 81
- Power to invest 81
- Power of apportionment 81
- Power to invade principal 82

Duties of the Trustee 83
- Duty of loyalty and good faith 83
- Duty of reasonable care and skill 83
- Duty to make property productive 84
- Duty to account 84
- Liability to third parties 84

Termination of the Trust 85
- Termination by the settlor 85
- Termination after the settlor's death 85
- Termination by the court 85

TRUSTS AND ESTATES GOVERNING LAW (*continued*)

Trusts Created by Operation of Law.........................87
- Resulting trust – failure or inadequacy of express trust.........87
- Purchase money conveyances.........87
- Constructive trusts.........88
- Fraud.........88
- Violation of fiduciary or confidential relationship.........89
- Secret trusts on testamentary transfers.........89

Review Questions.........93
- Multiple-choice questions.........93
- True/false questions.........95
- Answer keys.........98

EXAM INFORMATION, PREPARATION AND TEST-TAKING STRATEGIES.........99

Introduction to the Uniform Bar Examination (UBE).........101
- Structure of the UBE.........101
- The Multistate Bar Examination (MBE).........101
- Interpreting the UBE score report.........101
- The importance of the MBE score.........102
- MEE and MPT scores.........103
- The objective of the Multistate Bar Exam.........103

Preparation Strategies for the Bar Exam.........105
- An effective bar exam study schedule and plan.........105
- Focused studying.........106
- Advice on using outlines.........106
- Easy questions make the difference.........107
- Study plan based upon statistics.........108
- Factors associated with passing the bar.........108
- Pass rates based on GPA and LSAT scores.........109

Learning and Applying the Substantive Law.........111
- Knowledge of substantive law.........111
- Where to find the law.........112
- Controlling authority.........112
- Recent changes in the law.........113
- Lesser-known issues and unusual applications.........113
- Practice applying the governing law.........113
- Know which governing law is being tested.........114
- Answers which are always wrong.........114

EXAM INFORMATION, PREP & TEST-TAKING STRATEGIES (continued)

Honing Reading Skills 115
- Understanding complex transactions 115
- Impediments to careful reading 115
- Reading too much into a question 115
- Read the call of the question first 116
- Negative calls 116
- Read all choices 116
- Broad statements of black letter law may be correct 116

Multiple-Choice Test-Taking Tactics 117
- Determine the single correct answer 117
- Process of elimination 117
- Elimination increases the odds 117
- Eliminating two wrong answers 118
- Pick the winning side 118
- Distance between choices on the other side 118
- Questions based upon a common fact pattern 119
- Multiple true/false issues 119
- Correctly stated, but the inapplicable principle of law 119
- "Because" questions 120
- "If" questions 120
- "Because" or "if" need not be exclusive 120
- Exam tip for "because" 120
- "Only if" requires exclusivity 121
- "Unless" questions 121
- Limiting words 121

Making Correct Judgment Calls 123
- Applying the law to the facts 123
- Bad judgment equals the wrong answer 123
- Judgment calls happen 123
- The importance of procedure 124

Exam Tips and Suggestions 125
- Timing is everything 125
- An approach for when time is not an issue 125
- An approach for when time is an issue 126
- Difficult questions 126
- Minimize fatigue to maximize your score 126
- Proofread the answer sheet 127
- Intelligent preparation over a sustained period 127

EXAM INFORMATION, PREP & TEST-TAKING STRATEGIES (*continued*)

Essay Preparation Strategies and Essay-Writing Suggestions ... 129
- Memorize the law ... 129
- Focus on the highly tested essay rules ... 129
- Practice writing essay answers each week ... 129
- Add one essay-specific subject each week ... 129
- Make it easy for the grader to award points ... 130
- Conclusion for each essay question ... 130
- Tips for an easy-to-read essay ... 131
- Think before you write ... 131
- The ability to think and communicate like a lawyer ... 131
- Do not restate the facts ... 132
- Do not state abstract or irrelevant propositions of law ... 132
- Discuss all the issues raised ... 133
- Methods for finding all issues ... 133
- Indicators requiring alternative arguments ... 133
- Avoid ambiguous, rambling statements and verbosity ... 134
- Avoid undue repetition ... 134
- Avoid slang and colloquialism ... 134
- Write legibly and coherently ... 134
- Timing strategies ... 135
- Stay focused ... 135
- Law school essay grading matrix ... 135

APPENDIX ... 137

Overview of American Law (*diagram*) ... 139

U.S. Court Systems – Federal and State Courts ... 141
- Jurisdiction of federal and state courts ... 141
- Organization of the federal courts ... 143

How Civil Cases Move Through the Federal Courts ... 145
- Jury trials ... 145
- Bench trials ... 146
- Jury selection ... 146
- Instructions and standard of proof ... 146
- Judgment ... 147
- Right to appeal ... 147

APPENDIX (continued)

How Criminal Cases Move Through the Federal Courts 149
    Indictment or information 149
    Arraignment 150
    Investigation 150
    Deliberation and verdict 150
    Judgment and sentencing 151
    Right to appeal 151

How Civil and Criminal Appeals Move Through the Federal Courts 153
    Assignment of judges 153
    Review of a lower court decision 153
    Oral argument 153
    Decision 153
    The Supreme Court of the United States 154

Standards of Review for Federal Courts (*table*) 156

The Constitution of the United States (*a transcription*) 157
    Preamble 157
    Article I 157
    Article II 162
    Article III 164
    Article IV 165
    Article V 165
    Article VI 166
    Article VII 166

Enactment of the Bill of Rights of the United States of America (1791) 167

The Bill of Rights: Amendments I–X 169

Constitutional Amendments XI–XXVII 171
    Amendment XI 171
    Amendment XII 171
    Amendment XIII 172
    Amendment XIV 172
    Amendment XV 173
    Amendment XVI 173
    Amendment XVII 173
    Amendment XVIII 174
    Amendment XIX 174
    Amendment XX 174

APPENDIX (*continued*)

    Constitutional Amendments XI–XXVII (*continued*)

        Amendment XXI 175

        Amendment XXII 176

        Amendment XXIII 176

        Amendment XXIV 176

        Amendment XXV 177

        Amendment XXVI 178

        Amendment XXII 178

    States' Rights Under the U.S. Constitution **179**

        Selective incorporation under the 14th Amendment 179

        Federalism in the United States 179

Trusts and Estates Governing Law

Trusts and Estates are generally tested as a standalone subject and appear on the exam regularly. A question on wills or trusts will likely appear on the exam, but seldom both. Maximize your score by mastering the frequently tested Trusts and Estate items such as intestate succession, types of trusts (e.g., pour-over, discretionary, charitable), class gifts, future interests, validity and revocability of a will or trust.

Learn essential vocabulary to score more points on Trusts and Estates. Trusts definitions to know are settlor, beneficiary, trustee, testamentary trust, pour-over will, power of appointment, and rule of convenience. Wills definitions to know are ademption, codicil, descendant (or issue), devise or legacy (i.e., gift), disclaim, heirs, intestate, predecease, testate and testator.

The Probate Estate

Distribution of the estate

The law of wills, the rules of intestate distribution, and the laws governing estates' administration apply to the assets which are in the probate estate of the decedent.

The assets in the probate estate are held in the name of the decedent at the time of death.

The following property is not held solely in the decedent's name is not in the probate estate.

Partnership property

Partnership property, absent a specific provision in the partnership agreement, vests in the remaining partners at death.

The asset, which is in the estate of the deceased partner, is the right to an accounting of the value of the deceased's partnership assets.

Many partnership agreements modify this rule and permit the estate to remain as a partner or provide a mechanism whereby the deceased partner's interest is liquidated.

Property held in a fiduciary capacity

Property held by the decedent as a trustee (i.e., fiduciary) does not vest in the executor but must be turned over to the successor fiduciary.

Jointly-held property

Real and personal property held between the decedent and another as joint tenants or property held between the decedent and their spouse as tenants by the entirety passes directly to the surviving joint tenant. It is not part of the probate estate.

Completed gifts

An irrevocable gift made by the decedent during their lifetime, either outright or in trust, is vested in the donee or the trustee and is not part of the probate estate.

Causes of action – survival

Lawsuits pending and which survive death are assets of the probate estate.

Suits that survive death in which the decedent was a defendant can be prosecuted against the estate.

Contract actions and tort actions for personal injury survive death.

Intangible tort actions, such as libel, slander, and deceit, do not survive death. The estate cannot recover on such actions, nor is it liable for such actions brought because of actions of the decedent.

Causes of action – wrongful death actions

Actions to recover for the conscious pain and suffering and lost wages which the decedent suffered while living are assets of the probate estate.

Proceeds received from actions for wrongful death, while brought by the executor in the name of the decedent death actions, are not assets of the probate estate. These proceeds are distributed primarily to the surviving spouse and children per a statutory formula.

Life insurance and rights under pension plans

Insurance on the life of the decedent, even if the decedent was the owner of the life insurance policy, which is payable to a named beneficiary, is paid directly to the named beneficiary and is not an asset of the probate estate.

The decedent's pension plan proceeds, naming an individual as a beneficiary after the death of the decedent pass outside the probate estate.

Intestate Distribution of Estate

Complete and partial intestacy

Most exams have a question that requires applying the laws of descent and distribution.

The most common way for applying the law of intestacy is when an actor in a question dies without a will, and the examinee must determine how their estate should be distributed.

A complete or partial intestacy occurs when a will does not entirely dispose of the decedent's assets. This occurs if the will has no residuary clause or does not effectively dispose of the probate estate assets.

Even if an heir has been disinherited in the body of the will, they take by intestacy if the will fails to dispose of all assets.

The estate will be distributed by the intestacy law, where a will is declared invalid, and there is no prior will that governs the estate's distribution.

If a trust does not entirely dispose of its assets, which would occur when the final distribution is to the children or issue of a named beneficiary and that beneficiary does not have children or issue, the assets are disposed of by intestate distribution.

Intestate distribution laws are applied as if the settlor had died at the time when there was a failure of distribution, not at the time of the settlor's death.

Statutory disposition

The laws of intestate distribution apply to the net probate estate, which are assets remaining in the probate estate after the payment of debts, expenses of administration, funeral expenses, and taxes.

Spouse survives

Determining if a spouse survived the decedent presents two issues:

1) the person who claims the position of a surviving spouse must be validly married to the decedent and not divorced from the decedent when the decedent died, and

2) the person who was the spouse must survive the decedent. If their deaths were simultaneous, the simultaneous death act discussed below applies.

Spouse and issue survive

Issue includes the decedent's descendants whether, by blood or adoption, and includes children, grandchildren, great-grandchildren, etc.

If a surviving spouse and the decedent are survived by issue, that surviving spouse takes one-half of the net probate estate by intestacy.

The issue takes the other half per the rules for the distribution of the estate among the issue.

Spouse and kindred survive

If the decedent has a surviving spouse but no surviving descendants but is survived by kindreds (i.e., related persons to the decedent) such as parents, siblings, nieces, nephews, aunts, uncles, or cousins, the surviving spouse takes a statutory amount (e.g., the first $300,000) of the net probate estate and one-half of the remaining probate estate.

The kindred take half above the statutory amount.

For example, the decedent has a surviving spouse and a surviving mother and father, and the estate is $600,000. The surviving spouse takes $450,000 (statutory amount plus ½ in excess), and the mother and father take $75,000 each.

Spouse survives, but no issue or kindred survive

If a spouse survives without issue or kindred, the surviving spouse takes the entire probate estate.

Issue survive

If the decedent is survived by issue and there is no surviving spouse or the surviving spouse does not take their portion, the entire net probate estate is allocated to issue.

If children survive the decedent, that property reserved for issue passes in equal shares to the surviving children and to issue of any deceased child by right of representation.

If no children are surviving, the property is divided equally among grandchildren with a right of representation for the children of a deceased grandchild who is survived by issue.

No issue survive, but parents survive

If the decedent is not survived by issue, property not allocated to a surviving spouse is divided equally to the surviving parents.

No issue and no parents survive, but siblings or their issue survive

If there is no surviving issue or parents, property not allocated to a surviving spouse passes to the decedent's siblings, including half-siblings (i.e., persons with one parent in common with the decedent).

Issue of a deceased sibling, nephews, nieces, and their issue, take their deceased parent's share by right of representation as long as one sibling survives.

If there are no surviving siblings, property not allocated to a surviving spouse is inherited by nephews and nieces in equal shares with the issue of a deceased nephew or niece taking their parent's share by right of representation.

If those taking are in the same generation, they share equally; otherwise, they take equally in the older generation with children of deceased members of that generation taking their parent's share by right of representation.

No issue, parents, siblings, or their issue survive

If neither issue, parents, siblings, nor their issue survives, property not allocated to a surviving spouse passes in equal shares to the next of kin of the same degree of kindred.

The degree of kinship is determined by counting from the decedent up to the decedent's common ancestors and the next of kin and counting down to the next of kin.

For example, a first cousin is of the fourth degree of kindred because two degrees are used by counting to the common grandparent and two degrees counting down to the level of a cousin.

For example, a first cousin once removed is of the fifth degree of kindred.

For collateral kin of equal degree claim through different ancestors, those claiming the nearest ancestor are preferred.

Escheat

If a spouse and nor kindred survive, the property escheats to the state.

Additional rules of intestate distribution

A person adopted is a child of their adoptive parents for purposes of intestate distribution.

They take as an heir from their adoptive parents and the position of a child of their adoptive parents in determining their right to inherit from their adoptive parent's relatives.

An adopted child loses their status as a child of their natural parents when determining their right to inherit from them or their kindred.

The exception is that a child adopted by a spouse of a natural parent after the other natural parent dies retains the right to inherit from the relatives of the deceased natural parent.

When an adopted child dies intestate and is not survived by issue, their heirs are determined as if they had been born to their adoptive parents.

Half-blood

Children with one common parent are siblings for intestacy purposes and inherit an equal share with persons who have two common parents.

Children born out of wedlock

A child born out of wedlock is always a child of their mother for purposes of intestate succession, even if deemed an illegitimate child.

A child born out of wedlock is deemed a legitimate child of both parents for intestacy purposes if their parents have intermarried and the father has acknowledged them as his child or been adjudged as the father.

A child born out of wedlock who is illegitimate may inherit from and through their father:

> 1) if the father acknowledged paternity, or
>
> 2) if, during their lifetime or after death, the decedent has been adjudged in a judicial proceeding to be the father.

An illegitimate child may initiate a judicial proceeding to establish paternity after the decedent's death.

The descendants of a deceased illegitimate child may take their share by representation if paternity of the illegitimate has been acknowledged or established if paternity has not been acknowledged or judicially established, an illegitimate child cannot take as a child under intestacy laws.

If an illegitimate person dies intestate without issue, their mother or relatives are their heirs.

For their father and relatives to take by intestacy, the father–child relationship must be established by the father's acknowledgment of the child or through judicial proceedings.

Posthumous children

A child born to a married woman after her husband's death is a child of the deceased husband under intestacy laws.

The fatherhood of a child born out of wedlock after the father's death can be judicially established.

Limitation of rights of heir or legatee who kills testator

Some states have no statute which limits the rights of heir or legatees who kill the testator to inherit from their estate but imposes a constructive trust on the assets which such a person would receive and redistributes them to those who would inherit if the murderer predeceased the testator.

Notes for active learning

Execution of Wills

A will is a declaration of how a person wants their property to be distributed upon their death. It is a testamentary distribution of property. The person who makes the will is the testator or testatrix (if female). Every state has a Statute of Wills that establishes the requirements for making a valid will in that state.

Contract to make a will

A contract to make a will containing specific provisions is valid if it is in writing.

The consideration for such a contract is often that the other party will make a reciprocal will.

If the testator violates their contractual obligation by executing a will that does not contain the provisions obligated by contract, the will executed is valid, but the person holding the contractual obligation can impress the estate with a constructive trust to dispose of the assets following the contractual obligation.

A critical issue in many questions is the devolution of the property after death and assesses whether an instrument described in the question is a valid will.

To intelligently discuss that issue, apply the following law.

Age for capacity to execute a will

A person must be eighteen years of age or older to execute a valid will.

Testamentary capacity

The testator must be of sound mind; that is, must understand in a general way:

    1) the nature and extent of their property

    2) the natural objects of their bounty; and

    3) the nature of their act of making a will.

In a contest over the validity of a will, the will's proponent, usually the named executor, has the burden of proving that the testator was of sound mind when the will was executed.

The testator is presumed to be of sound mind until the opponents of the validity of the will introduce credible evidence that the testator lacked testamentary capacity.

The proponent of the will has the burden of persuasion on the issue and must prove capacity by a preponderance of the evidence.

In such a will contest, three classes of persons are competent to give an opinion on the soundness of the testator's mind when the will was executed:

1) witnesses to the will;

2) the testator's physician; and

3) a psychiatrist or other person who can qualify as an expert on sanity.

Other persons may testify in a will contest concerning facts upon which conclusions about the testator's sound mind can be based.

Testamentary intent

For a document to be a valid will, the testator must sign it with the understanding of making a will.

A document is ineffective as a will if the testator intends that it is a joke or solely designed to accomplish some purpose other than disposing of their property at death.

If the testator executes a will conditioned on some event occurring and it does not occur, the will is revoked.

The testator must generally know and approve the contents but need not know the technical details contained in it.

Written requirements for the execution of a valid will

A will must be entirely in writing.

A nuncupative will (an oral disposition of personal property) may be used only by a soldier in actual military service or a mariner at sea.

Oral wills are otherwise invalid.

Signature required by the testator or at their express direction

The writing must be signed by the testator or another in their presence and express direction.

If the testator intends the writing to be their signature executing the document, which they assert as their will, the testator may sign or make a mark on any part of the will.

Proper attestation

Holographic wills are entirely in the testator's handwriting and not valid unless attested or executed in a jurisdiction that recognizes the validity of unattested holographic wills.

The testator's signature must be properly attested to by two witnesses.

The testator need not sign the instrument in the presence of the witnesses.

If the testator does not sign in their presence, the testator must show their signature to each attesting witness, acknowledge that the signature is theirs, and ask them to sign the will as attesting witnesses in the testator's presence.

The will is valid even if a witness did not see the testator's signature if the witness could have seen it if they had wished.

The witnesses must know that they are witnessing a will but need not read it or be aware of its contents.

A competent witness can be any person of enough understanding when a subscribing witness, even if a minor.

A person who affixes the testator's signature to the will at their express direction may serve as a witness to the will.

A will is valid even if the witness is dead or incompetent when offered for probate.

The witness's signature can be proven by persons who saw them sign the will or identify the witness's signature.

At a probate proceeding where the validity of the will is in issue, the witness need not have a present memory of executing the will if they identify their signature as a subscribing witness.

The witnesses do not have to reside in the jurisdiction where the testator is domiciled.

Interested witnesses

Most jurisdictions stipulate that interested parties, such as a beneficiary or the attorney who drafted the will, cannot be witnesses. If an interested party has attested to a will, state law either voids any clauses that benefit such person or voids the entire will.

A person who signs the will as one of the two necessary attesting witnesses and receives a legacy or devise under the will is an interested witness.

The fact that the witness was interested does not invalidate the will.

The legacy or devise to an interested witness or an interested witness's spouse is void.

If there are more than two witnesses to the will, the interested witness's signature is superfluous, and the legacy to that witness is valid.

If the witness is not named a legatee or devisee in the will but takes because of an anti-lapse statute's operation, their legacy is valid.

A witness is not considered an interested witness because they are named executor but receives no legacy of a will.

He does not forfeit their appointment as executor because they witnessed the will.

The signature of a person as a witness to a will who is an officer or director of a charity named a beneficiary of the will does not void that charity's legacy.

If a legacy is void because the legatee was a necessary witness to the will, that legacy is treated like a lapsed legacy. An alternative legatee takes, or if there is no alternative legatee, the residue is increased by the void legacy.

If the void legacy is the sole residuary legacy, or there is no residue clause in the will, the amount of the void disposition is distributed per the laws of intestacy.

If there is more than one residuary legatee, and the legacy to one of them is void because that residuary legatee was an interested witness, the residuary legatee is divided among the other residuary legatees proportionately unless the will indicates a contrary intent.

Codicils

Once a will has been validly executed, it cannot be altered or amended except by an instrument executed following the requirements for a valid will.

If the testator changes the content of the will on the face of the will by adding a new legatee or substituting one legatee for another, the changes are invalid, and the will, as initially executed, will be considered the testator's will.

An exception to this rule is the doctrine of partial revocation.

If the testator only crosses out a specific part of the will, that act is considered a partial revocation of that portion.

A will can be changed by a codicil (i.e., a document that alters an existing will) executed with the same formalities as a will.

A codicil modifies rather than replaces the will's provisions unless a contrary intent is clear.

A validly executed codicil republishes the will on the codicil's date.

A challenge to the original will cannot be sustained unless the challenge is also effective against the codicil.

A properly drafted codicil should explicitly refer to the will.

Revocation and Revival of Wills

Will revocation

Even if it is concluded that a will is valid, determine that it has not been revoked before using its provisions to dispose of the decedent's estate.

Events in the testator's life such as marriage and divorce occurring after the will is executed and before death revokes a will either wholly or partially.

The voluntary action of the testator may revoke a will in two ways.

Revocation by an instrument executed in the same manner

The testator can revoke a will by another instrument executed and attested to in the same manner as a will.

The instrument that frequently revokes a will is a subsequent will that typically contains language explicitly revoking prior wills and codicils.

The subsequent instrument may contain no dispositive language and only contain language revoking prior wills, in which case the intestacy laws would govern the estate's devolution.

If an instrument revokes part of a will, it is considered a codicil.

If the subsequent will is not valid, it does not revoke the earlier will.

Revocation by intentional destruction

The testator may revoke a will wholly or partially by performing a physical act on the will itself to revoke it in whole or in part.

Crossing out specific paragraphs of a will is a partial revocation of those sections.

If the testator, with intent to revoke a will, causes physical destruction of the paper by tearing or burning it, the entire will is revoked.

Defacing the will by writing canceled over the writing in the document revokes it.

An unwitnessed notation signed by the testator declaring the will revoked is not enough.

There is a presumption that a will that cannot be found was revoked.

That presumption can be rebutted by producing secondary evidence of its contents and showing that the testator did not intend its destruction.

The scrivener can testify to the contents of the will because the attorney-client privilege is inapplicable in probate proceedings dealing with a will's validity.

Intentional destruction of one of two duplicate wills constitutes a revocation.

Conditional or dependent relative revocation

If the revocation of a will occurred by a physical act conditioned upon the valid execution of a new will, the new will is not valid because it was improperly executed. The revocation is not valid, and the old will continues to be operative.

Revival of revoked wills

A will that has been revoked by a subsequent will is not automatically revived if the subsequent will is thereafter revoked.

If the testator's intent at the time they revoked the subsequent will is to reinstate a prior will, the court will revive the prior will.

Special Circumstances Affecting Intestate and Testate Distribution

Simultaneous death

The Uniform Simultaneous Death Act applies if the order of death of two or more individuals cannot be determined by affirmative proof.

If there is valid forensic evidence or eyewitness testimony that one person lived longer than the other, this Act does not apply.

The Act applies to the interpretation of the effect of wills and the application of intestacy laws.

Its Act's provisions are frequently tested in Wills' questions.

The mechanics of its operation should be committed to memory.

The basic principle of the Act is that in determining a person's estate whose death coincided, conclusively presume that the decedent survived the other person whose death coincided.

Thus, inconsistent facts are applied to the estate of each decedent.

The specific rules are:

    1) A legatee or devisee in a will or a person entitled to take under the intestacy laws who died simultaneously is deemed to have predeceased the decedent whose estate is being distributed. Therefore, the rules of lapsed legacies apply.

    2) If the two persons who died simultaneously held property as joint tenants or as tenants by the entirety, then for one half of the property, one joint tenant is deemed to have survived, and the second joint tenant is deemed to have survived for the other half.

    Half of the jointly held property is considered an asset of the estate of each who died simultaneously. That estate is probated as if the holder of the other half of the joint tenancy has predeceased them.

    3) The named beneficiary in an insurance policy predeceased the insured.

The insurance policy proceeds would thus be payable to the alternative beneficiary or the deceased's estate if there is no alternative beneficiary.

For a question involving simultaneous deaths, determine which assets, including jointly held assets, are in the estate of each decedent and determine how the estate is to be distributed as if the other person who died simultaneously had predeceased the decedent.

Advancement

Property which the decedent gives during their lifetime to an heir, with the intent that the gift satisfies wholly or partially the share to which the donee would be entitled from the donor's estate is an advancement.

The amount of the *inter-vivos* gift is added to the intestate estate. The larger amount is divided by the number of shares in the estate to determine each beneficiary's amount.

The amount of the advancement is deducted from the share of the heir who received it.

An *inter-vivos* gift is an advancement only if the donor describes the gift as an advancement in writing or if the donee acknowledges the gift as an advancement in writing.

The advancement is its fair market value at the date of the gift or the amount in which the donor states the value to be at the date of the gift.

Renunciation of property interests

A person may disclaim in whole or in part any interest passing to them as the result of the decedent's death by filing a signed disclaimer in probate court (and in the registry of deeds where disclaimed realty is located) within the statutory time (e.g., nine months) after the donee became entitled to the property.

Once filed, a disclaimer is irrevocable and becomes the property of the person who would have taken it if the disclaiming party had died immediately before the event, which entitled the disclaiming party to receive the property.

Limitations on testamentary dispositions

The decedent's right to make an effective testamentary disposition is limited by considerations of public policy set forth in statutes.

Spouse's elective share

In wills questions requiring to determine which individuals take which parts of the estate, always consider the rights of a surviving spouse to take an elective share and compare the size of that share to the amount which the surviving spouse would take under the will.

Property that the spouse receives as a surviving joint owner or from the proceeds of an insurance policy or through *inter-vivos* gifts does not count against their elective share.

A surviving spouse has a statutory right to waive the provisions of the will and claim the statutory elective share.

This right must be exercised by a writing filed in the Registry of Probate within the statutory time (e.g., six months) after the decedent's will has been allowed.

The spouse's elective share (calculated on the net probate estate) is computed by one of three formulae depending on the other heirs.

To file for an elective share, the person claiming to be the surviving spouse must be validly married to the person claiming to be the surviving spouse at the time of their death and not be a party against whom a separate support action has been filed.

If issue survive

If the decedent is survived by issue, the spouse takes one-third of the net probate estate.

If the amount of the net probate estate is more than $75,000 so that the elective share would exceed $25,000, the spouse receives only $25,000 outright and a life interest in the amount by which the one-third share exceeds $25,000.

The spouse receives a life estate in the portion of the estate, which is real property, and a life interest in a trust fund for the remaining amount in which they are entitled as a life interest.

If kin survive, but no issue survive

If the decedent is survived by kin but no issue, the spouse takes the first $25,000 of the net probate estate outright, plus the income from one-half of the remaining probate estate.

If no issue or kin survive

If the decedent is not survived by issue or kin, the spouse takes $25,000 outright plus one-half of the remaining probate estate outright.

If a spouse has deserted the decedent spouse, or in a case where the decedent spouse was living apart from the surviving spouse under a probate decree of separate support for a justifiable cause, the spouse has no right to waive the will.

The right to waive the will and take a statutory forced share is personal to the spouse and terminates if they die before waiving the will.

The will may not be waived by the executor of the surviving spouse's estate.

Acceptance of any benefits under the will bar the right to waive.

Property held in a revocable *inter vivos* trust where the decedent was settlor, sole trustee, and life income beneficiary is part of the probate estate for purposes of computing the amount of the estate to which the election statute applies.

Some states do not have a statute that calculates the amount to which the waiver statute applies by including jointly held property, completed *inter-vivos* gifts, proceeds of life insurance, and the value of property held in trust for the benefit of the deceased spouse.

When making the waiver-of-the-will calculation, not all states deduct the amounts contained in the above categories, which are now the property of the surviving spouse.

Children not mentioned in the will (pretermitted children)

In will fact patterns where the decedent is survived by a child or by the children of a deceased child, who is not mentioned in the will, consider the possibility that the child is pretermitted (i.e., not mentioned in the will) and has the right to claim their intestate share.

A child can be pretermitted whether born before or after the date when the will was executed.

There are three ways in which a testator can prevent a child or grandchild of a deceased child from being pretermitted.

1) He can leave the child or grandchild a legacy of any size.

2) The testator can indicate that the omission was intentional and not caused by mistake. The easiest way to show intent is to state that intent in the will.

3) He can make provisions for that child during their lifetime.

The terms "accident" or "mistake" do not refer to facts that led the testator to omit the child intentionally but instead to error or mistake in drafting and executing the will.

For example, if the testator says that they make no provision for Son because Son stole from them, Son is not a pretermitted child even if the testator was mistaken about the theft.

The executor and the persons who oppose the child's claim have the burden of showing that the omission was not caused by accident or mistake.

The pretermitted child must file a claim against the estate for their intestate share.

No pretermitted child can take a share in real property unless a claim is filed in the Registry of Probate within one year after approval of the executor's bond.

The intestate share paid to the pretermitted child is first paid out of the estate's residue and from devisees and legatees proportionally.

An illegitimate child cannot be a pretermitted child.

No limitations on charitable bequests

Some states have no statutory provisions limiting the proportion of an estate that may be left to charity nor limiting charitable bequests made in a will executed close to death.

Provisions in restraint of marriage

The testator cannot validly require that a legacy be forfeited if the beneficiary marries.

The testator can condition a testamentary disposition upon a legatee not marrying a person outside of their religion.

Courts are likely to construe a provision that appears to be an absolute restraint on marriage as a provision for a beneficiary's support while that beneficiary is single.

Such a provision in a trust which supports a beneficiary until that beneficiary is married would be upheld.

Notes for active learning

Interpretation and Construction of Wills

Incorporation by reference

A will may incorporate a document, even ones not executed with the formalities of a will if it:

1) was in existence when the will was executed and

2) is identified by clear and satisfactory proof as the paper referred to in the will.

The doctrine has been expanded by statute for revocable *inter vivos* trusts.

The dispositive provisions of an existing revocable *inter vivos* trust may be incorporated by reference into a will even though the trust is revocable or amendable.

If the trust is amended after the will is executed, the document incorporated into the will is the trust as amended.

The devise or bequest to the trustee of a revocable *inter vivos* trust lapses if the trust is revoked or terminated before the testator's death.

Facts of independent significance

A will may provide for the designation of a beneficiary or the amount of a disposition by reference to some future unattested act occurring after the execution of the will if the future act has some significance apart from the will.

For example, a bequest of "one week's wages to those persons in my employ at the date of my death" has two facts that control the recipients' identity and the amount they are to receive, which will be determined after the will has been executed.

Each of these two facts has significance outside of the will itself.

Alterations and interlineations

A new provision inserted after a will was duly executed is invalid, but the will remains valid.

For alterations to the text of the will, they are valid if made before the will was signed.

The proponents of the will have the burden of proving that the alterations were made before the will was signed.

If the testator has struck out a provision of the will after the will was signed, that provision is revoked because a will may be wholly or partially revoked by defacing the instrument itself.

Ambiguities

Extrinsic evidence to explain or contradict the terms of a will is inadmissible unless the will is ambiguous, even if the language of the will was contrary to the intent which the testator expressed orally.

Patent ambiguities

Patent ambiguities appear on the face of the will. For example, the same parcel of property is devised for two different beneficiaries in two separate paragraphs of the will. Extrinsic evidence is not admissible to resolve such ambiguity. The instrument is construed from its language alone or according to general rules of construction.

A mistake may cause the patent ambiguity in the *factum*, a mistake in the will itself, such as an inaccurate description of the property or an erroneous identification of legatee.

Usually, a will may not be corrected for a mistake in the *factum*.

The testator refers to a person (e.g., "my wife"), but the language does not accurately describe their legal relationship; the court will ignore the erroneous legal description.

Latent ambiguities

Latent ambiguities occur when there is no inconsistency in the language of the will itself, but extrinsic facts give rise to ambiguity.

For example, the will may devise $20,000 to Aunt Angela. The testator had two aunts named Angela because their mother and father each had a sister named Angela.

Where there is such a latent ambiguity, extrinsic evidence is admissible to aid in interpreting the will.

Construction of Terms for Relationship and Survivorship

Heirs and next of kin

The terms *heirs* and *next of kin* ordinarily mean persons who inherit by intestacy at the time of the decedent's death.

If the time for the interest of heirs or next of kin to vest is later, the terms include persons who would have been the decedent's heirs at that later date.

For example, if the testator devises a life estate "to my wife for life and then to my heirs," the heirs are those who would have taken if the testator had died at the time that the life estate in the testator's wife terminated.

Then living

The term *then living* requires that the person taking the remainder interest be alive when the prior estate terminates.

Adopted children

Unless a contrary intent plainly appears by the instrument's terms, adopted children are treated the same as natural children in construing the words "child," "grandchild," "issue," "heir," or "heir-at-law."

Construction of devises

If a will devises real estate and does not specify the quality of the estate conveyed, the devise is in fee simple or, if the testator cannot devise a fee simple, the greatest estate the testator could devise.

Exercise of a general power of appointment

The residuary clause of a will does not exercise a general power of appointment held by the testator unless it shows an intent to exercise that power.

If the general power of appointment is not exercised, the assets of the trust in which the power of appointment was held will go by way of the provisions of the trust controlling a default in the exercise of the power of appointment.

If there is no default provision, the property in the trust would go to the heirs of the settlor determined as of the time of the failure to exercise the power of appointment.

Notes for active learning

Changes in Property, Beneficiaries and Marital Status Before Death

While the will is executed during the testator's life, it does not become operative until death.

During that time, changes can occur in the testator's marital status, the testator's property, and the individuals who are beneficiaries of the will.

Each of these changes affects how the will disposes of property at the death of the decedent.

Classification of testamentary dispositions

Testamentary dispositions are classified per the assets of the estate available to pay them.

A specific devise or bequest disposes of an identified item of property owned by the testator and, except in extraordinary circumstances, can only be paid by delivering that asset.

A demonstrative bequest is a gift payable primarily from a specified source and, if that source is inadequate, the estate's general assets can be used to pay it.

A general or pecuniary bequest is payable from the estate's general assets rather than requiring distribution from specific assets.

A residuary disposition is a gift of whatever remains in the estate after claims and other dispositions have been satisfied.

Effect of change in assets between execution and death

The property, which is the subject of a specific bequest, is adeemed, and the beneficiary receives nothing if the testator does not own that asset at the time of death.

Specific bequests – ademption by extinction

An item purchased to replace the asset is not the subject of the specific bequest.

For real estate, which is subject to a binding purchase and sale agreement at the time of death, the doctrine of equitable conversion applies, and the asset of the estate is the right to the proceeds, not the real estate.

An exception to the ademption rule is if the testator's conservator or guardian sold the property.

In that example, the beneficiary is entitled to anything that remains of the proceeds of the sale.

Pecuniary bequests – ademption by satisfaction

If the testator gives a prospective legatee a gift before the will is executed, that gift will not be considered to have satisfied a bequest.

If a gift is received by a beneficiary from the testator after the will is executed, it will only be considered to have satisfied the bequest if the testator declared in writing that it was in satisfaction of the gift or unless the beneficiary acknowledged in writing that the gift was in satisfaction of the bequest.

The rule is like that of advancements for intestate shares.

Changes in securities

A legatee is only entitled to the number of shares of the security as has been bequeathed to them, providing that the testator owned that many shares at death.

The legatee is entitled to additional shares of security if the testator received them as a stock split or stock dividend from the original shares bequeathed.

The specific legatee is entitled to securities received in exchange for the bequeathed securities due to a merger, consolidation, reorganization, or similar action.

Encumbered property

The devisee of real property or the legatee of personal property takes the property subject to any mortgage or security interest at the time of death unless the will provides differently.

Lapse – changes in beneficiaries

Unless the will provides an alternative disposition if the named beneficiary predeceases the testator or unless the anti-lapse statute applies, a legacy or devise made to one who predeceases the testator lapses.

If the lapsed legacy is not a residuary, the amount of that legacy becomes part of the estate's residue and passes under the residuary clause.

If the lapsed legacy is the residuary legacy, the assets pass by intestacy.

The anti-lapse statute

When an anti-lapse statute is applicable, the legacy which was supposed to go to a deceased beneficiary is transferred to the issue of that deceased beneficiary provided that the testator has not shown a different intent.

The anti-lapse statute is only applicable when the deceased beneficiary is a blood relative of the testator.

A gift to the deceased child of a spouse does not pass by operation of the anti-lapse statute to the issue of that child.

For the anti-lapse statute to operate, the deceased relative must have been survived by issue, including adopted children.

The property passes to the issue per the law of intestate distribution discussed above.

For example, if the beneficiary were survived by two children and the two children of a deceased child, the children take one-third of the legacy. The remaining one-third would be split between the children of the deceased child.

The legacy is not paid under the will of the deceased relation.

If the deceased blood relative survived by issue dies before the execution of the will, the anti-lapse statute will still apply.

If there are two or more residuary legatees and one predeceases the testator, the remaining legatees take the residue, and nothing is distributed by intestacy.

If the deceased residuary legatee is a relation and is survived by issue, the anti-lapse statute applies, and the issue takes the deceased residuary legatee's share of the residue.

Class gifts – definition of a class

A class gift exists when a testator makes a gift to several persons, usually with the same relationship to the testator, such as "nephews and nieces."

The class may increase in number as additional persons are born and qualify as members of the class, or it may decrease as members of the class die before the time the gift is to be distributed.

Whether a group of beneficiaries is to be considered a class or to be considered individually is answered by determining the intent of the testator.

Time to determine membership

If the class gift is a legacy or devise to be paid at the time of the testator's death, membership in the class is determined at the testator's death.

Persons who have predeceased the testator, even if they were alive at the time of the will, are not members of the class.

Even if they bear an appropriate relationship to become class members, persons born after the testator's death are excluded.

If the class gift is payable at some time after the testator's death, the time for determining membership in the class is the time when the property is distributed to the class.

Unless there is a provision in the will that conditions the benefits of the class gift upon survivorship until distribution time, membership in the class does not decrease after the testator's death. However, it can increase with births after death but before distribution.

If distribution of the benefits of the class gift takes place over time (e.g., beneficiaries are eligible for distributions when they obtain a specific age), the rule of convenience, which can be overcome by expressing a contrary intent, closes class membership at the first distribution.

The anti-lapse applies to class gifts.

If the testator left the property 'to my brother for life and his children," the statute allows the issue of the testator's nephews and nieces who predeceased the testator to take.

However, if the provision were "to my brother for life and then to his children then living," the anti-lapse statute could not apply because there is a condition of survivorship.

Changes in marital status – marriage

Marriage after the date of the execution of the will revokes an entire will unless it appears from the will itself that it was made in contemplation of the marriage.

Unless such a testator makes a new will after marriage, their estate is distributed by intestacy laws.

A will revoked by marriage is not revived by divorce.

Changes in marital status – divorce

A divorce or annulment revokes provisions in a will for the former spouse, and the property passes as if the former spouse had predeceased the testator.

A divorce revokes the designation of the former spouse in a fiduciary capacity under the will.

If the testator remarries their former spouse, the provisions are revived.

A legal separation of spouses does not terminate their married status and does not revoke any provisions of a will.

Community property

States such as Arizona, California, Idaho, Louisiana, Nevada, New Mexico, Texas, Washington, and Wisconsin recognize a form of co-ownership known as community property. This method of co-ownership applies only to married couples and is based on the notion that a husband and wife should share equally in the fruits of the marital partnership. Under these laws, each spouse owns an equal half share of the income of both spouses and the assets acquired during the marriage regardless of who earns the income. Property acquired through gift or inheritance before or during the marriage remains separate property. When a spouse dies, the surviving spouse automatically receives one-half the community property.

The other half passes to the deceased spouse's heirs as directed by the will or by state intestate statute if there is no will. Neither spouse can sell, transfer, or gift community property during the marriage without the other spouse's consent.

Upon divorce, each spouse has a right to one-half of the community property. The location of the real property determines whether community property law applies. For example, if a married couple who lives in a noncommunity property state purchases real property located in a community property state, community property laws apply to that property.

Notes for active learning

Governing Law

The Distribution of The Estate After Death

The estate at the time of death

Most exam questions require explaining how the estate of the decedent is distributed at death.

The will, which was ambulatory until the time of death, becomes an operative instrument by the process of probate.

A petition to probate the decedent's last will and testament is filed by the executor in the probate (e.g., county) court of the decedent's domicile at the time of death.

The burden of proving that the will was validly executed, that it has not been revoked, and that the decedent was competent at the time of execution is on the proponent of the will.

The decree admitting the will to probate established the will as the decedent's probate estate's dispositive instrument.

The decree may be revoked if a later will is found or the will was a forgery.

The named executor is ordinarily appointed executor when the will is allowed, but the court has the discretion to appoint a different fiduciary if the named executor is unfit.

If there is no will, the probate process is known as administration.

The surviving spouse has the first claim on the fiduciary position of the administrator.

Children have the next right to the appointment as administrators.

The administrator performs duties like an executor and distributes the estate following the laws of intestacy.

Will contests

The decedent's heirs and beneficiaries of a prior will have standing to contest the validity of the will offered for probate on one or more of three grounds.

The heirs must be given notice of the petition for probate.

Legatees under prior wills should be given notice if their existence is known, but failure to notice prior legatees will not void the probate proceeding.

A testator may include a valid and enforceable provision in their will requiring any legatee who contests the will to forfeit any provisions made under the will.

A beneficiary petition for interpretation of a will does not challenge the validity of the will and therefore does not invoke an *in terrorem* clause.

Improper execution

If the will was improperly executed, it is invalid.

Improper execution will occur if the testator fails to sign the will in the presence of witnesses or acknowledge to them that the signature on the will is theirs or the statutory number of witnesses (e.g., one, two) fail to attest to the will.

The named executor has the burden of proving proper execution.

Lack of testamentary capacity

The validity of the will may be challenged if the decedent was under age 18 when the will was executed or if they were not of sound mind.

The burden is on the proponents to establish a sound mind once those challenging the will have produced credible evidence of an unsound mind.

Undue influence

A ground for challenging the will is that the testator was under undue influence at execution.

To constitute undue influence, coercion (mental, physical, or moral) must cause the desires of the person accused of using undue influence to be incorporated into the will rather than the desires of the testator.

Kindness or care for the decedent does not constitute undue influence if the testator responds by giving such person a substantial legacy.

If the person accused of exerting undue influence is in a fiduciary relationship to the testator and benefits themself, the court will likely find undue influence.

Legacies in favor of the scrivener of the will are particularly suspect.

The contestant bears the burden of proving undue influence.

Fraud in the inducement

Fraud, which deprives the testator of their right to make a will based upon the true state of affairs, is of two types, fraud in the inducement and fraud in the factum.

Fraud in the inducement is a knowingly false representation that causes the testator to make a different will than otherwise.

If successfully proven, fraud in the inducement will only void those provisions of the will, which were the product of that fraud, and the remaining portions of the will can be probated.

If the testator, in the absence of fraud, makes a mistake not having to do with the execution of the will, which induces them to dispose of property in a particular manner, the will is valid.

For example, a mistake about the value of one's property, or concerning how the decedent has been treated by one of their relatives, or whether the natural object of one's bounty is living or dead will not invalidate the will.

The test for determining whether the testator had sufficient mental capacity to create a valid trust is typically like that required to make a valid will. To have capacity, the settlor must have been at least 18 years old and must know the extent of their property and the natural objects of their bounty. The "natural objects" include family members such as spouses, children, and siblings.

Fraud in the *factum*

Fraud in the factum occurs when the decedent is defrauded that they are making a will or about the contents of the will.

For example, the decedent thinks they are signing a contract when the document is a will, or the decedent signs a will but does not know that there are beneficiaries in the will whom they did not want.

For it to be the basis to contest a will, the fraud must be operative when the will was executed.

The burden of proving fraud is on the contestant.

Fraud in the *factum* goes to whether the decedent knew that they were executing a will and voids the instrument.

Remedies for fraud and undue influence

A person objecting to a will based on fraud or undue influence must contest the validity of the will in probate and cannot maintain a separate action for constructive trust or tort damages.

If the fraud or undue influence prevented the execution of a will in favor of the plaintiff, they would maintain a tort action for interference with an advantageous relationship.

If the alleged wrongdoer benefited from their conduct by taking under the decedent's will, the remedy for the person who was left out of the will is to ask the court to impose a *constructive trust* upon the defendant's ill-gotten gains for the plaintiff's benefit.

A constructive trust is not an actual trust by the traditional definition; a constructive trust is a legal fiction remedy for unjust enrichment.

The constructive trust orders the unjustly enriched person to transfer the property to the intended party.

Other reasons for the invalidity of a will

The probate court, where the will is probated, is the forum to address other issues concerning the validity of the will, such as whether the will has been revoked or terminated by a subsequent marriage.

If the court determines that a will is invalid for any reason, prior wills may be probated since the provision in the invalid will revoking prior wills is invalid.

If there are no prior wills, the court treats the probate as an administration and distributes property by the laws of intestacy.

Issues altering the operation of the will

The probate court is the forum where the issues of pretermitted children and waiver of the will by a surviving spouse are determined.

Collection of the assets of the estate

Once appointed, the executor or administrator collects the estate assets and files an inventory.

Special rules affect the following assets.

Debts owed by the executor to the estate

Any debt which the executor owes to the estate is treated as paid.

The executor must account for that money in their final account.

If the executor cannot pay it and they filed a surety bond, the sureties must pay the amount the executor owed the estate.

Income from specifically bequeathed assets

Income-producing assets specifically devised or bequeathed carry the right to income from the date of death.

The executor is entitled to the income accrued to the decedent before death as a general asset of the estate.

Income accruing after death is paid to the beneficiaries of the specifically bequeathed assets.

Real estate – heirs or devisees normally have control

Real estate descends directly to the heirs or devisees, and the executor does not have the right to rents nor the responsibilities of management as soon as the will is allowed.

Executor may sell real estate to pay debts and expenses

If the estate's personal property assets are insufficient to pay debts and taxes of the estate, the executor has the power to petition the probate court to sell real estate to satisfy obligations.

To give good title to real estate during the first year after the death, a license from the probate court for the executor to sell with the assent of the devisees is necessary.

Powers and duties of a fiduciary

Unless the will or a probate court order confers greater authority, the executor or administrator has limited power.

The executor may expend money to protect and preserve estate assets and comply with the decedent's contractual obligations.

To liquidate the estate, the executor has the power to sell personal property.

If the estate is solvent, the executor or administrator can keep the assets that the decedent held and distribute assets in kind or partly in kind.

Standard of executor's obligations

An executor or administrator is a fiduciary and subject to fiduciary duties of care and loyalty

Liability of executor or administrator

An executor is not personally liable for contracts made by them in their capacity as an executor unless they failed to reveal their fiduciary capacity.

A creditor may hold the estate liable on such contracts.

The estate, but not the executor, is liable in tort due to control of the estate's property unless the executor is personally negligent.

To satisfy the duty of care, an executor must carry liability insurance on managed property.

Payment of debts and claims

The executor or administrator first uses the estate assets to pay debts and claims in the following order of priority.

A widow's allowance (payable immediately after death without regard to the estate's debts) to help the widow and minor children adjust to death has priority on the assets.

The amount is per minor child given with a limited amount for necessaries for the widow.

A widower would probably qualify for such an allowance.

The priorities for debts are in the following order:

1) expenses of administration;

2) necessary funeral expenses and expenses of last illness;

3) debts entitled to preference under laws of the United States;

4) taxes and excise duties;

5) wages (up to statutory amount) for labor performed within a year of death;

6) debts for necessaries furnished to the decedent or their family within 6 months of death;

7) all other debts.

If the assets are insufficient to satisfy one class in full, the debts abate pro-rata.

Priority of secured debts with collateral

A secured party, including a mortgagee, may seek repayment out of the security and is not subject to priorities except the extent to which the debt exceeds the collateral value.

Suits for services – claimant can testify

Since some states have no dead man rule, plaintiffs can testify to an oral contract with the deceased for services.

If the claim is for services rendered, only claims accruing during the last six years of the decedent's life are collectible because of the statute of limitations.

Claim to leave property by will

If the claim is that services were rendered in reliance on an oral promise to leave the property by will, the suit on the contract to leave the property by will is unenforceable because of the statute of frauds.

The plaintiff can sue the estate and collect damages in *quantum meruit* for the fair value of services rendered in reliance on the unenforceable oral promise.

The cause of action for a promise to leave the property by will does not accrue until the will becomes operative at the time of death.

The contract statute of limitations will not bar a claim for services rendered in reliance on the promise, and the plaintiff can collect for services rendered after the date of the promise if the estate is sued promptly.

Debts due to the executor

If the executor has a claim against the estate, they may collect it.

The beneficiaries have a right to contest the validity and amount under arbitration procedures established by the probate court.

Notice of claim filed against an estate

A creditor should make a claim by mailing a written statement of the claim to the executor within the statutory period (e.g., four months) after the executor or administrator has been appointed, describing the nature and extent of the claim.

Disallowance of claims

The executor or administrator has a statutory period (e.g., sixty days) after receipt to disallow the claim.

Failure to disallow gives that claim the status of an allowed claim and tolls the statute of limitations for suits against estates.

Payments during the statutory period

Because the executor or administrator does not know the number of claims against an estate, the executor should not pay claims within the statutory period (e.g., four months) from their appointment.

If the executor pays claims they have knowledge of after the statutory period, they are not personally liable to creditors who make a later claim, which would render the estate insolvent.

Statute of limitations for suits against the estate

Suits against the estate, except for the exceptions discussed hereafter, must be brought within the statutory period from the deceased's death.

Notes for active learning

Exceptions to One-Year Statute for Suits Against the Estate

The Supreme Court may permit a late-filed claim if it finds the claimant is not guilty of culpable neglect and that equity and justice require the waiver.

New assets in an estate

If new assets come into the estate more than one year after the decedent's death, creditors may sue for the new assets within six months after the executor receives them or four months after the creditor learns of them, whichever comes first.

Claim not yet accrued

If a claim is presented before the estate is fully administered but will not accrue during the one year, the court may order that sufficient assets be held to satisfy the claim when it matures, and the lawsuit need not be commenced until the cause of action accrues.

Claim satisfied out of insurance

If the claim is to be satisfied by an insurance policy or bond, the suit may be brought within the time limits of the ordinary statute of limitations if that suit is within three years of the date of death.

Tax returns

The executor is responsible for paying the federal estate tax and filing estate tax returns if the estate is large enough to require that a return be filed.

The executor must file fiduciary income tax returns to report the income earned by the estate.

Notes for active learning

Payment of Legacies and Distributive Shares

Payment to a spouse in intestacy without issue

The administrator must pay a statutory amount to the spouse first out of personalty and then from the realty in an intestate administration where a spouse, but no issue survives.

If the entire net probate estate is less than the statutory amount, the administrator can obtain a determination that the surviving spouse is entitled to the entire estate.

Time of the payment of legacies

Legacies are not payable until a statutory period (e.g., nine months) after the executor's appointment.

General or pecuniary legacies carry interest after the statutory period elapses.

A legacy to support a minor or widow instead of a dower bears interest from the date of death.

Income earned from the date of death from a bequeathed asset is paid to that beneficiary.

Legacies to executor, debtors, and creditors

A legacy to a person named as an executor ordinarily requires that the executor serves in that capacity to qualify for the legacy.

Whether a bequest left to a creditor of the estate is used to reduce the debt owed is determined by the intent of the testator.

The size of the bequest, the relationship between the creditor and testator, the character of the legacy, and the time the debt arose are relevant factors in making that determination.

If the testator is a creditor of the legatee, the executor has the right to offset the debt against the legacy unless the legatee shows that the testator intended to forgive the debt and grant a legacy.

If the statute of limitations barred the debt at the time of the execution of the will, there is a strong indication that the testator did not intend that it be collected.

Abatement of legacies

The testator has the power to specify the order in which legacies will abate where the assets are insufficient.

If the assets of the estate are insufficient to pay the creditors and legacies in the will, the order of abatement is:

1) residuary legacies;

2) general legacies which abate *pro-rata* if not enough assets exclusive of specific legacies to pay them in full;

3) specific legacies and devises that abate pro-rata if specific legacies and devises must be used to satisfy the estate's debts.

Legacies satisfying a legal obligation of 1) the testator, 2) a minor, 3) instead of dower, or 4) as the result of an ante-nuptial agreement, are entitled to priority over specific legacies and devises.

Completion of the Administration of the Estate

Filing account

Upon complete administration of the estate, the executor or administrator files a final account, showing inventory, income, expenses, and distributions.

Challenge to account

Heirs and other interested persons have a right to challenge the account.

If found deficient, the executor can be required to pay sums into the estate, and the sureties can be held liable if the executor defaults.

Finality of account

Once allowed, the executor is discharged and is subject to further challenge only if the allowance of the account was procured by fraud or manifest error.

Notes for active learning

Conflict of Laws for Wills

Domicile

The domicile determines intestate succession to personal property.

If the will is in writing and is signed, a will executed in conformity with either the law of the testator's domicile or the law of the place where it was executed will be recognized as a valid will by state court.

If the decedent who executed a will out of state dies domiciled in the state, the construction and legal effect of a disposition of personalty are governed by state law; and the disposition of real estate is governed by the law of its *situs* of that real estate.

A choice-of-law provision in a will specifying that a specific state's law will govern it will be recognized unless the law of a different state is contrary to public policy.

The decedent is most familiar with the laws of their domicile.

Attorney consultations would most likely be conducted in the domicile.

The domicile state bears the burden of intestate distribution.

The domicile of the decedent is used to choose the law to be applied to determine the intestate succession of personal property.

Domicile at death determines which state gets estate taxes.

The law of the *situs* determines intestate succession to real property.

Conflicting domicile determinations – the states apply their standards for determining domicile and may separately rule that a party was domiciled in their respective state (a legal impossibility).

Dorrance v Martin et al. (1935) – two states imposed estate taxes after deciding that the decedent was domiciled in their respective state.

The imposition of multiple state estate taxes violates the due process clause only if the taxes exceed the value of the estate. To avoid additional tax, an intent to change domiciles should be done thoroughly and quickly.

Choice of laws application

For land, the law of the *situs* applies.

Movable property – law of the *situs*, but issues arise (e.g., the *situs* of stock certificate).

Personal property – the domicile of the decedent at death.

The policy governs the status of property *vs.* determining who takes under a will (*situs* rule fractionalizes estate but might be consistent with expectations).

For wills, it might be better to look at domicile at the time of execution.

Intestate succession is determined by domicile. Domicile is determined by the law of the forum and requires physical presence and intent to remain indefinitely.

Modern rule – domicile depends on the issue (old rule: unitary).

White v. Tennant (WV 1888) (moved from PA to WV but for less than one day): domicile was established upon arrival.

Estate of Jones (Iowa 1921) (Lusitania): death in transit uses the previous domicile until "new domicile is secured."

Model Execution of Wills Act, which provides that the testator will subscribe to a written document shall be valid as to matters of the form if it complies with the local requirements of several enumerated states.

Definition of a Trust

Trusts divide legal and equitable interests

A trust is an entity recognized by the law in which a trustee holds legal title to the property to benefit the beneficiaries who have an equitable interest in the trust property.

Separation of the legal and equitable title is an essential element of a trust.

If a sole trustee who holds the legal interest is identical to the sole beneficiary holding the equitable interests, there is a merger.

The trust is terminated, and the sole trustee/beneficiary owns the property outright.

An essential element of a trust is that the trustee stands in a fiduciary relationship with the beneficiaries concerning the trust property.

Distinguished from other relationships

Agency, debtor-creditor, and bailment distinguish between trust and other legal relationships.

The facts may be ambiguous in some questions, so discuss the law of trusts and analyze the facts under one of the following legal frameworks.

Agency

A trust is distinguished from an agency because an agent does not hold legal title to the principal's property.

Debtor–creditor

A trust is not a debtor–creditor relationship.

A creditor has a claim at law against the debtor for damages in the amount of the debt. In contrast, a trust beneficiary has an equitable interest in specific trust property and the benefit of the trustee's fiduciary obligations.

Bailment

A bailee only has a possessory interest, not title, in the property held for the bailee.

While the bailee has a duty to avoid negligence concerning the property and can be required to turn the property over to the bailor, there is no fiduciary duty between the bailor and bailee.

Notes for active learning

Voluntarily Created Trusts

Methods of trust creation

A voluntary trust is created when the settlor with the express or implied intent to create a trust performs the acts necessary to establish a trust.

The acts of the settlor may be donative or required by a contractual relationship.

The act which accompanies the creation of a trust is a *declaration* or *transfer*.

Trust creation by declaration

A trust is created by a declaration when the settler, orally or in writing, intends to hold property that they own in trust and hold it at least partially for others' benefit.

When a declaration creates a trust, the settlor is the trustee, and the settlor holds legal title to the property in their fiduciary capacity as trustee.

Trust creation by transfer

A trust can be created when the settlor transfers the legal title to their property to a third party and designates the beneficiaries who have the equitable title to the property.

Voluntary or donative trusts

A voluntary trust is created without consideration by declaration (or transfer).

A declaration needs communication of the intent to hold property in trust and does not need to comply with the formalities of a transfer.

Thus, an individual can make an effective gift in trust by declaring that they are holding property, which they own in trust, for the benefit of the donee of the gift without the need of delivery to complete the gift.

If a transfer is necessary to complete the creation of a voluntary trust, the settlor must comply with the delivery requirements for a donative transaction to be complete.

Personal property must be delivered to the trustee.

There must be execution and delivery of a deed to the trustee for a trust to be created by the transfer of real property

A voluntary declaration of trust requires a clear showing of intent to create a trust.

If the declaration of trust is oral, there must be notice to and acceptance by the beneficiary.

No notice to a beneficiary is needed with a written declaration of trust.

Trusts created by contract

If there is an obligation to create a trust by a contract supported by valid consideration and that obligation is specifically enforceable, the person who has agreed to create a trust can be required in equity to satisfy their obligation and transfer the property to a trust.

If the promise involves a trust where the *res* (body) of the trust is land, the contract will have to be enforceable under the statute of frauds.

Testamentary or *inter vivos* trusts

A testamentary trust is created in a will and becomes operational only at death.

An *inter vivos* trust becomes effective during the lifetime of the settlor.

Pour-over provisions for testamentary trusts

A trust created by the terms of a will is only valid if the will is valid and can only be amended by a subsequent will or a codicil.

Under the doctrine of incorporation by reference, the estate assets may be bequeathed or devised to an existing inter-vivos trust.

This trust is known as a pour-over trust.

By statute, if the trust is in existence when the will is executed, the trust can subsequently be amended by the testator in a manner that does not observe the formalities of executing a will. The assets poured into the trust will be governed by the terms of the amended trust.

An *inter vivos* trust is irrevocable unless the settlor expressly retained the power to revoke it.

If a settlor attempts to set up a trust that will only come into existence at their death, it must be created by an instrument executed with the formalities of a will.

If the trust is created during the lifetime of the testator, it will not be invalid because it did not comply with the formalities of wills even if the settlor is the sole trustee, the sole lifetime beneficiary, and retains the power to amend and revoke it.

Such a trust is the classic pour-over trust commonly used today.

Savings account trust

A common substitute for a testamentary disposition is a savings bank trust where the donor opens an account in their name in trust for the donee.

There must be a formal document setting forth the terms of the trust, or the donor must give notice to the beneficiary that the trust has been created.

Gifts to minors

The Transfers to Minors Act allows the registration of certain types of personal property in a custodian's name for a minor.

The custodian may make payments for the minor's use and benefit without court approval, and the property becomes the sole property of the minor upon reaching majority.

Notes for active learning

Required Elements of a Trust

For a private voluntary trust to be validly created, the following elements are necessary

Once created, a trust will not fail for lack of a trustee because the courts can always appoint a successor trustee if no trustee is named in the instrument.

Capacity of the settlor

The settlor must be of sufficient age and mental capacity.

If the trust is testamentary, the validity of the trust depends upon the validity of the will.

The capacity of the testator/settlor can be challenged in a will contest.

The creation of an *inter vivos* trust requires a present capacity of the settlor to declare that they are holding property in trust or conveying the trust property.

The settlor must convey the present intent to create a trust relationship where the legal title to the property is held by a trustee for the benefit of a beneficiary and must comply with the formalities of creating a trust by declaring themselves trustee or transferring the property to a trustee.

To create a trust, the language employed by the transferor settlor when transferring the property to a transferee must impose mandatory obligations on the transferee to hold the property in trust for the benefit of the trust beneficiaries.

If the transferor uses precatory language such as "wish," "hope," "request," or "desire" for the transferee's use of the property, they will not create a trust due to the lack of an enforceable obligation placed upon the transferee.

Where the circumstances show that the settlor did intend to impose mandatory duties, a court may construe precatory language as creating mandatory obligations on the transferee and therefore creating a trust.

In making that determination, the court may be more likely to find a trust if the settlor had an obligation to support the beneficiaries.

Necessity for writing

A testamentary trust is part of a will and must always be created by formally executed writings.

An *inter vivos* trust may be created orally if it involves only personal property.

An *inter vivos* trust containing land created by a settlor's declaration is valid only if the settlor has executed a writing indicating that they are holding the land in trust.

If the trust in land is created by transfer to the trustee, that transfer must be in writing.

If a purported settlor conveys land to a third person without indication that the third person holds the property in a trust, the transferee can carry out the terms of the trust that were given by the trustee orally or void any trust obligation.

An oral promise to hold proceeds from the sale of land in a trust is not within the Statute of Frauds and will be enforced when the trustee sells the property.

Trust property

There must be some identifiable trust property in which the settlor can declare that they hold in trust or with a present right to convey to a trustee.

Intangible property interests and contingent interests, which are more than mere expectancy, can be the subject of a trust.

Definite or ascertainable beneficiaries

For a private trust instead of a charitable trust discussed later, the beneficiaries must be identified or ascertainable.

The settlor may designate a definite and ascertainable class of persons as beneficiaries.

Valid trust purpose

A private express trust cannot be created for an illegal purpose or contrary to public policy.

If the trustee, in carrying out the terms of the trust, would be required to commit a tortious act or defraud creditors of the settlor, the trust is invalid.

Time restrictions

The Uniform Statutory Rule Against Perpetuities provides that the interest of the beneficiaries in the principal of a trust, or a special, testamentary, or contingent power of appointment is valid if it is certain to vest within the common-law rule period or does vest within 90 years after its creation.

The statute embodies a wait rule, which allows the non-vested property interest a grace period of 90 years to vest.

The statute has a reformation provision that allows a court on the petition of an "interested person" to modify an invalid disposition under the rule stated above so that it follows the grantor's intent as nearly as possible but does, in fact, vest within 90 years.

Defining Characteristics of Charitable Trusts

Charitable purpose

A legally recognized charitable purpose, such as the furtherance of health, religion, education, government, or the arts, is an essential characteristic of a charitable trust.

The settlor can create a charitable trust that does not set forth a defined charitable purpose but limits the trustees' activity to the furtherance of charitable purposes.

Indefinite class of beneficiaries

For a trust to qualify as charitable, there must be a public benefit, so the persons to be benefited must be members of an indefinite class.

If a defined class of beneficiaries such as a scholarship trust at a university for the settlor's descendants, the trust is not charitable.

If the class of beneficiaries is large such as the inhabitants of a specific town, the indefinite class of beneficiaries' test has been met.

Similarities to private trusts

A charitable trust may be created by any methods for creating an express trust, and there must be a settlor with the capacity to convey properly expressed intent, and a specific trust *res* (or *corpus*), and power of enforcement.

Notes for active learning

Limitations of Private Trusts Inapplicable to Charitable Trusts

Rule against perpetuities inapplicable

A charitable trust may continue indefinitely and is not subject to the rule against perpetuities or the rule against accumulations unless the accumulation is found to be unreasonable.

Failure of purpose

When some other change in circumstances renders it impracticable to administer the trust as provided by the settlor, or the charitable purpose intended by the settlor has or can no longer be accomplished, the doctrine of *cy pres* (as near as possible) may be applicable.

Instead of terminating the trust, the courts alter the trust's purpose to continue while following the settlor's original intent as possible.

Under the *cy pres* doctrine (i.e.., *amending a legal document*), a court may modify the trust's purpose and permit the trustee to use the trust *res* (body) for another charitable purpose, close to the settlor's original charitable intent.

If the trust instrument indicates that the *cy pres* doctrine is not applied, the trust *res* (i.e., body) reverts to the settlor or their estate.

Enforcing the trust

In a private trust, the beneficiaries have the power to enforce the provisions of the trust.

Since there are no defined beneficiaries in a charitable trust, the enforcement power is given by statute to the state's Attorney General.

Notes for active learning

Spendthrift Provisions

Protections for beneficiaries

A beneficiary's equitable interest in income or principal of the trust may be voluntarily assigned and may be subjected to the claims of judgment creditors of the beneficiary unless the terms of the trust provide otherwise.

The settlor may insert a spendthrift provision in a trust, which validly prohibits the beneficiary from transferring their interest in the trust before it is distributed to them.

Such a provision prevents the beneficiary's creditors from reaching the beneficiary's interest in the trust to satisfy their claims.

Once a beneficiary receives a distribution from the trust, creditors may reach that distribution.

A settlor cannot insert a spendthrift provision in a trust which protects their beneficial interest in the trust from creditors.

A discretionary trust, in which the beneficiary has no right to income until the trustee decides to pay it, will so protect the beneficiary's interest from creditors.

The settlor can give the trustee the discretionary power to pay income due to a specific beneficiary or accumulate it and provide that the trustee has the discretion to pay the income among several beneficiaries.

When those provisions are in place, neither the beneficiary nor their creditors can compel payment or funds from the trust.

Notes for active learning

Administration of the Trust by the Trustee

Appointment of the trustee

The settlor ordinarily has the power to select the trustee and provide for succession of trustees.

If the trustee refuses to serve or fails to qualify, the probate court has broad discretion in naming a trustee or appointing a successor trustee to fill a vacancy.

Resignation or removal of the trustee

Once a trustee is in office, they may resign if authorized by the trust instrument or with permission of all the beneficiaries or the probate court.

The probate court has the power to remove a trustee upon a petition filed by the beneficiaries for failing to perform their duties, breaching a fiduciary duty, or where there is hostility between the trustee and the beneficiaries.

Compensation of the trustee

A trustee is entitled to receive reasonable compensation for their services as a trustee.

A trustee is entitled to reimbursement for expenses occurring in the administration of the trust.

A trustee who is an attorney can render legal services to the trust and be paid separately for those services.

If the trust instrument does not allocate fees between income and principal, the court can determine the allocation.

Notes for active learning

Powers of the Trustee

The trustee has powers conferred by the trust instrument to manage the trust assets and distribute them to beneficiaries; the trustee may incorporate statutory optional fiduciary powers by reference.

Power of sale or contract

Without a specific grant of power, a trustee may sell and transfer personal property unless the trust instrument prohibits such sale.

The authority to sell or transfer real estate must be expressly granted in the trust.

Otherwise, the trust must obtain court approval to sell or transfer real estate.

A trustee has the power to enter contracts on behalf of the trust and further has the power to execute instruments that will accomplish or facilitate the exercise of their other powers.

Power to invest

A trustee has the power and duty to invest the trust property, make the property productive, and use reasonable care and skill to choose and manage investments.

Power of apportionment

If the trust provides that income is paid to one set of beneficiaries and principal to another set, the trust instrument sets the standards for apportionment of income and expenses.

Absent authority in the trust instrument, the trustee should pay ordinary expenses out of income and extraordinary expenses and those solely beneficial to the remainder interests out of principal.

The general rule provides that cash dividends are allocated to income and stock dividends to the principal.

Power to invade principal

The trust instrument can provide discretionary principal payments to income beneficiaries and usually set up a standard by which such payments should be made.

The discretion of the trustee to make such payments will rarely be disturbed by a court.

Unless there is power in the trust instrument to invade principal, a court will not permit principal payments to an income beneficiary if the instrument benefits a different principal beneficiary.

If an income beneficiary is the sole principal beneficiary upon a particular age, the court has the discretion to permit principal payment acceleration for circumstances not foreseen by the settlor.

Duties and Liabilities of the Trustee

Duty of loyalty and good faith

The highest fiduciary duty of loyalty is imposed upon a trustee.

The trustee must avoid conflicts of interest between their interests and the trusts and between the interests of others to whom the trustee owes a fiduciary duty and those of the trust.

When a conflict occurs, the trustee cannot enter a transaction on behalf of the trust unless the transaction is fair to the trust and the trust instrument authorizes them explicitly, or the trustee makes appropriate disclosure and receives permission from the court or beneficiaries.

If a beneficiary is not competent to act, guardian *ad litem* should be appointed and act on behalf of the incompetent beneficiaries.

If the trustee takes an action that affects life tenants and remaindermen, the trustee must act fairly to each group.

If the trustee purchases property in their individual capacity, which is an appropriate opportunity for the trust, a constructive trust can be imposed upon the property held by the trustee in their individual capacity.

A constructive trust can be imposed upon the property if the trustee purchases property from the trust without complying with their fiduciary obligations.

Duty of reasonable care and skill

The trustee must abide by the limitations imposed by the trust instrument for their powers of investment.

The trustee must exercise reasonable care and skill in managing the trust.

The trust instrument can authorize the trustee to take greater risks with trust investments and particularly authorize the trustee to retain the investments transferred initially to the trust even though the investment concentration would not be prudent for trust investment.

If the trustee exercises the required standard of care, they are not liable for mistakes in judgment.

Unless the trust instrument authorizes delegation explicitly, a trustee may not delegate their duties to others, except for ministerial (i.e., purely administrative) duties.

Even though a trustee can seek expert advice on matters concerning trust property, the trustee must supervise agents and make the final decision on actions suggested.

Trust property must not be commingled with the trustee's property.

Except when there is an authority to invest in a common trust fund, it should not be placed with funds from other trusts.

Duty to make property productive

The trustee may not keep unproductive property such as vacant land as an asset of the trust unless the trust instrument authorizes this or the beneficiary's consent for such an investment.

The trustee has a duty to sell the unproductive property and reinvest in productive assets.

Duty to account

The trustee has a duty to account to the beneficiaries, telling them how they managed the trust property, the income they are entitled to, and the amount of principal held in the trust.

Liability to third parties

A trustee is not personally liable for a contract, which they make in a disclosed capacity as a trust unless the contract expressly provides personal liability.

A trustee is not personally liable for torts committed during prudent administration of the trust unless there is a personal fault by the trustee.

The trust estate is liable for claims in tort or contract for obligations entered by the trustee or tort claims arising from the trust's property.

Termination of the Trust

Termination by the settlor

The settlor's unilateral action could terminate a trust if they reserved the power in the trust instrument to revoke it.

If the power is not reserved, the trust cannot be terminated by the settlor unless they obtain all the beneficiaries' consent, which must be of legal age and competent.

Termination after the settlor's death

Even if all the beneficiaries of a trust approve of its termination after the settlor's death, courts will not ordinarily terminate it before the time specified in the trust if such termination is contrary to the settlor's intent.

Where no material purpose of the settlor remains to be accomplished, the court may allow termination upon request of all the beneficiaries whose interests are vested and who are competent to consent.

If the trust is spendthrift or discretionary, the settlor's purpose in creating the trust has not been fulfilled, so it cannot be terminated even if all the beneficiaries desire such termination.

The trustee has no power to terminate the trust unless such power was expressly granted.

If the trustee has the power to distribute the principal of the trust, they can effectively terminate it by conveying the trust property to the beneficiaries per the terms of the trust.

Termination by the court

If an emergency or unforeseen circumstance (e.g., severe medical need) by a beneficiary causes the trust purpose to be impaired or frustrated, a court may terminate the trust even though the settlor's material purpose still exists, and beneficiaries do not consent.

Notes for active learning

Trusts Created by Operation of Law

There are two kinds of legal entities labeled as trusts, purchase money *resulting trusts* and *constructive trusts* created by operation of law, and do not fit the classic definition of trusts.

Each entity is important for exam purposes because candidates must be aware of the circumstances where they are operative and discuss them in their answers.

Resulting trusts – failure or inadequacy of express trust

If the settlor failed to create an express trust and has transferred the property to an individual whom they intended to act as a trustee or the settlor has transferred the property to the trustee above that needed to accomplish the purposes of the trust, that person holds the property for the settlor, heirs, or successors.

The trust is a resulting trust because it is presumed that, upon the failure of an express trust or the lack of need, the settlor intended the property be retained for their benefit.

If a trust were created because of a contractual obligation of the settlor, the trust could fail.

If the person intended to be benefited by the contractual obligation creating a trust becomes the legal owner of the property rather than a beneficiary, no resulting trust was created.

If the settlor used precatory language when they transferred property, so no trust exists, and the transferee of the property holds the property outright, and no resulting trust exists.

Purchase money conveyances

When one person pays consideration for the transfer of property, but the title is taken in the name of another person, and there is no donative intent on the part of the person paying the consideration, the person receiving the property holds it in a purchase money resulting trust.

If the person named who furnished the consideration has an obligation to support the person whose name title is taken, the presumption for a gift and no resulting trust arises.

The presumption of a gift arises where one spouse furnishes the consideration for the purchased property, and the title is taken in the name of the other spouse.

No such presumption of a gift occurs if a parent furnishes the consideration and title is taken in the name of an adult child

Even where there is a presumption of a gift, that presumption may be rebutted by clear and convincing evidence, and a resulting trust arises.

The statute of frauds does not apply to a resulting trust.

Proof of the intent not to make a gift and not to vest a beneficial interest in the grantee of the deed may be made by parol evidence.

A resulting trust must arise at the time of purchase from a third party.

If the person furnishing the consideration takes the title from the seller in their name and subsequently transfers property upon an oral promise of the grantee to hold the property in trust, no resulting trust is presumed.

If the person who did not take title paid only part of the purchase price, they might establish a resulting trust for a partial interest in the property if they show clear and convincing evidence that their payment was for a distinct interest in the property.

Constructive trusts

A court creates a constructive trust as an equitable remedy when there is no intention (express or presumed) to create a voluntary trust.

The equitable remedy is employed to avoid unjust enrichment where the legal title to the property was obtained:

1) by fraud,

2) in violation of a fiduciary or confidential relationship,

3) by testamentary devise or intestate succession when the titleholder promised the testator that they would hold the property in trust for the benefit of someone else.

When a court finds that a constructive trust has been established, it will order the person whose conduct caused the constructive trustee to transfer title to and possession of the property held in the constructive trust to its rightful owner.

The circumstances which give rise to a constructive trust may be proven by oral evidence.

Neither the statute of frauds nor the parol evidence rule prevents a constructive trust from arising.

Fraud

If the property is conveyed to a person who makes a promise to use the property for a specific purpose and that person had no intent of fulfilling that promise when the property was conveyed, a court will impose a constructive trust upon the property requiring the grantee to use it for the intended purpose.

If the constructive trust remedy is not available because the grantor cannot prove an express trust and that the conveyance was procured by fraudulent intent, the grantor can recover the fair market value of the land based on a failure of consideration.

Violation of fiduciary or confidential relationship

A constructive trust will be imposed upon the property that is obtained in violation of a fiduciary relationship, such as attorney and client, trustee and beneficiary, physician and patient, business partners, employer and employee, corporate director or officer, and corporation or accountant and client.

Abuse of the fiduciary relationship can be shown by evidence of self-dealing or using confidential information to the advantage of the recipient at the expense of the one who disclosed the information or corporate opportunity.

Family relationship alone does not create fiduciary relationships but can be a factor if establishing one.

A fiduciary relationship does not ordinarily exist between businesspersons in arm's length relationships, but a confidential or fiduciary relationship may exist between those in a business relationship; if there is a misuse of confidential information.

Secret trusts on testamentary transfers

If a decedent fails to make a will and dies intestate, an express trust cannot be established.

If a decedent makes a will benefit an individual in reliance upon the oral promise of the person benefited by the will or by the intestacy that they use the inheritance to benefit another person, an express trust cannot be established.

A court can impose a constructive trust on the inheritance and require that the legatee use the property for fulfilling the promise made to the testator.

Relationship matrix

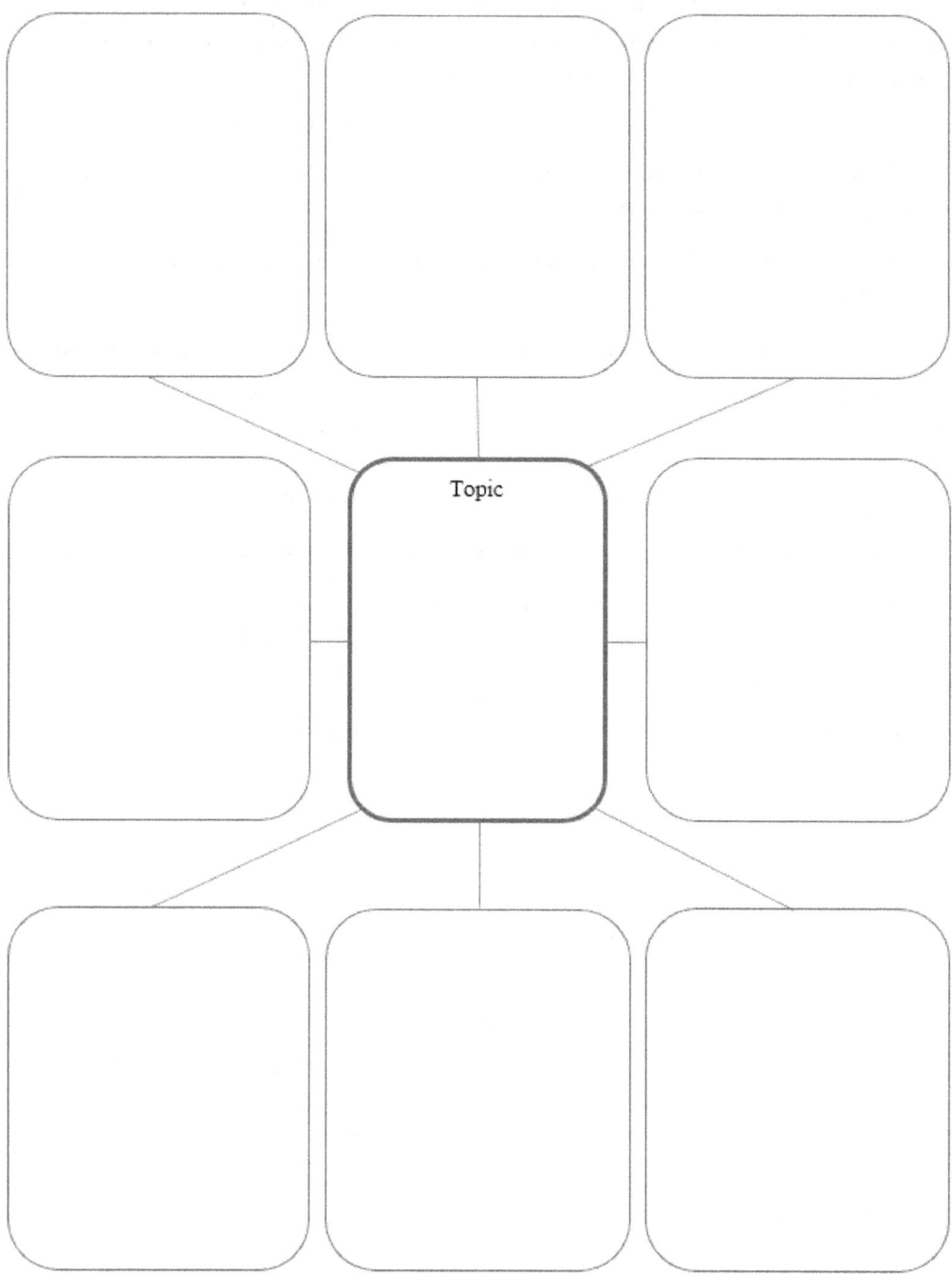

Notes for active learning

Notes for active learning

Review Questions

Multiple-choice questions

1. The type of trust created in a will is a:

   A. Testamentary trust
   B. *Inter vivos* trust
   C. Implied trust
   D. *Causa mortis* trust

2. The person who makes a will is the:

   I. Testator
   II. Testatrix
   III. Grantor

   A. I only
   B. I and II only
   C. III only
   D. I, II and III

3. The following methods can revoke at least part of a will:

   I. A subsequent will
   II. A divorce
   III. A codicil

   A. I only
   B. I and II only
   C. I and III only
   D. I, II and III

4. Testamentary capacity means that the person making the will must:

   A. Be of legal age and sound mind
   B. Be witnessed before two witnesses
   C. Sign or initial every page
   D. Have considerable assets

5. "To my beloved husband, I give you $500" is what type of gift?

   A. Residuary
   B. Specific
   C. Remainderman
   D. General

6. Intestate succession involves determining:

   A. Intestate property
   B. Heirs
   C. Estate property
   D. Escheat

7. Under the doctrine of ademption, the beneficiary:

   A. Is exempt from paying estate taxes
   B. Receives property remaining after taxes and creditors
   C. Renounces claim to inherited property
   D. Receives nothing

8. A will must, generally, be attested to by:

   A. The testator
   B. An attorney
   C. Competent witnesses
   D. Evidence of videotaping

9. A trust designed to prevent the beneficiary's creditors from getting the trust assets is a:

   A. Charitable trust
   B. Intestate trust
   C. Spendthrift trust
   D. Termination trust

10. If a testator leaves his red Ferrari to his former wife and the yellow Ferrari to his girlfriend, and at his death, the yellow Ferrari had been sold, which doctrine applies?

    A. Abatement
    B. Ademption
    C. Recidivism
    D. Bequestability

11. The legal way to make changes to an existing will is through a(n):

    A. Abatement
    B. Amendment
    C. Codicil
    D. Power of attorney

12. "If my niece has predeceased me, then I give my 1954 Aston Martin to my nephew" is what type of gift?

    A. Residuary
    B. Specific
    C. Bequestability
    D. General

13. A person on their deathbed may make the following type of will:

    I. Deathbed will
    II. Dying declaration will
    III. Nuncupative will

    A. I and III only
    B. II only
    C. III only
    D. I, II and III

14. A gift *causa mortis* is:

    A. Made in contemplation of death
    B. Dependent upon contract formation
    C. Given during a person's lifetime
    D. Irrevocable

15. When a testator distributes the same amount to all descendants, this method of gifting is:

    A. Arbitrary and unfair
    B. Fair and equitable
    C. *Per-stirpes*
    D. *Per-capita*

16. A residuary gift means:

    A. A gift of the top twenty-five percent of the estate holdings
    B. A portion of every gift distributed
    C. A gift of anything left after other distributions
    D. A gift of the homestead

17. The following is NOT required to make a will:

    A. Testamentary capacity
    B. Writing
    C. Self-proving clause
    D. Testator's signature

18. The elements that courts examine to determine undue influence include:

    I. The will contains a substantial benefit to the beneficiary
    II. The beneficiary assisted in the execution of the will
    III. The will has a distorted disposition of the testator's property

    A. I only
    B. I and II only
    C. I and III only
    D. I, II and III

True/false questions

19. A holographic will is captured in computer memory.

    True   False

20. The person who makes the will is the *testatum*.

    True   False

21. An *inter vivos* trust can be changed at the decision of the settlor.

    True   False

22. "*I hereby give to my administrative assistance my Cross pen*" is a specific gift.

    True   False

23. Generally, wills need not be in writing to be valid.

    True   False

24. Lineal descendants share equally without the degree of relationship for distribution *per stirpes*.

    True   False

25. A codicil must be executed in the same manner as a will.

    True   False

26. Gifts in a will can be specific, general, or residuary.

    True   False

27. Electronic recordings can supplement and strengthen a will.

    True   False

28. A holographic will must be in writing.

    True   False

29. A will may be revoked if the testator intentionally burns or tears the will.

    True   False

30. Attestation is when a will is adjudicated by a legal process to distribute property.

    True   False

31. Generally, an inheritance may not be renounced.

    True   False

32. A living will allows for the health care proxy to commit euthanasia.

    True   False

33. A nuncupative will must include the testator's signature.

   True   False

34. Most jurisdictions allow interested parties to act as witnesses to the will.

   True   False

Answer keys

1: A
2: B
3: D
4: A
5: D
6: B
7: C
8: C
9: C
10: B

11: C
12: A
13: D
14: A
15: D
16: C
17: C
18: D

19: False
20: False
21: True
22: True
23: False
24: False
25: True

26: True
27: True
28: True
29: True
30: False
31: False
32: False

33: False
34: False

Bar Exam Information, Preparation
and
Test-Taking Strategies

Introduction to the Uniform Bar Examination (UBE)

Structure of the UBE

The Uniform Bar Examination (UBE) includes 1) the Multistate Bar Examination (MBE), 2) Multistate Essay Examination (MEE), and 3) Multistate Performance Test (MPT).

The MBE has 200 multiple-choice questions accounting for 50% of the UBE.

The MEE has six essays worth 30% of the UBE score.

The MPT has two legal tasks (e.g., complaint, client letter) for 20% of the UBE score.

The Multistate Bar Examination (MBE)

The Multistate Bar Examination consists of 200 four-option multiple-choice questions prepared by the National Conference of Bar Examiners (NCBE).

Of these 200 questions, 175 are scored, and 25 are unscored pretest questions.

Candidates answer 100 questions in the three-hour morning session and the remaining 100 questions in the three-hour afternoon session.

The 175 scored questions are distributed with 25 questions on each of the seven subject areas: Federal Civil Procedure, Constitutional Law, Contracts, Criminal Law and Procedure, Evidence, Real Property, and Torts.

A specified percentage of questions in each subject tests topics in those subjects.

For example, approximately one-third of Evidence questions test hearsay and its exceptions, while approximately one-third of Torts questions test negligence.

Interpreting the UBE score report

Overall score. The National Conference of Bar Examiners (NCBE) states the Uniform Bar Exam (UBE) requires a passing scaled score between 260 to 280. Scores above 280 receive a passing score in every UBE state.

The "percentile" is the number of people that scored lower. If an examinee scored in the 47th percentile, they scored higher than 47% of the examinees (and lower than 53%).

The examinee is first given a "raw score,"; based on the number of correct answers.

The raw score is adjusted by adding points to achieve the "scaled score." The number of points added is determined by a formula that compares the difficulty of the current exam to prior benchmark exams.

The comparative performance of examinees on "control questions" (prior pretest questions) given on previous exams form the basis for determining each exam's difficulty.

MBE scaled score. Examinees receive a scaled score and not an MBE "raw" score (i.e., the number of correct answers). MBE scores are scaled scores calculated by the NCBE through a statistical process used for standardized tests.

According to the NCBE, this statistical process adjusts raw scores on the current exam to account for differences in difficulty compared to previously administered exams. The scaled score is calculated from the raw score, but the NCBE does not publish the conversion formula.

Since the MBE is a scaled score, equating makes it impossible to know precisely how many questions must be answered correctly to receive a particular score. Equating allows scores from different exams to be compared since a specific scaled score represents the same level of knowledge among exams.

The MBE is curved, so just because a score is "close" to passing does not mean you are close. For example, a 124 may be in the 31st percentile and a 136 in the 62nd percentile. A 12-point difference in scaled scores equates to a 31-point percentile difference. If you are in the 120s, much preparation is needed to increase your score.

For most states, aim for a scaled score of 135 to "pass" the MBE. If you are unsure what score you need, divide the passing score by two. For example, if a 270 is needed to pass the bar, divide 268 by two to yield 135 as a threshold score on the MBE.

The importance of the MBE score

A passing MBE score depends on the jurisdiction. In jurisdictions that score on a 200-point scale, the passing score is the overall score. Passing scores are often approximately 135.

For the July 2020 bar exam, the national average MBE score was 146.1, an increase of 5 points from the July 2019 national average of 141.1.

For comparison, on the July 2018 bar, the national average MBE score was 139.5, a decrease of about 2.2 points from the July 2017 national average of 141.7.

How much the MBE contributes depends on the jurisdiction. Each jurisdiction has its policy for the relative weight given to the MBE compared to other bar exam components.

For Uniform Bar Examination (UBE) jurisdictions, the MBE component is 50%.

Most jurisdictions combine the MBE score with the state essay exam score.

The overall state candidates' performance on the MBE controls the raw state essay's conversion to scaled scores. Achieve a scaled MBE score of at least 135 to pass the bar.

MEE and MPT scores

In a UBE score report, there are six scores for the Multistate Essay Exam (MEE) and two for the Multistate Performance Test (MPT). Most states release this information.

Most states grade on a 1–6 scale (some use another scale).

In states grading on a 1–6 scale, 4 is considered a passing score.

The MEE and MPT sections are not weighted equally.

The MEE essays are worth 60%, while the MPT is 40% of the written score.

Many examinees assume that they passed the MPT and MEE portions of the exam. Examine the score report to see how you performed on these portions.

The objective of the Multistate Bar Exam

Working knowledge of the MBE objectives, the skills it tests, how it is drafted, the relationship of the parts of an MBE question, and the testing limitations provide you a substantial advantage in choosing the correct answers to MBE questions and passing the bar.

Knowing which issues are tested and the form in which they are tested makes it more manageable to learn the large body of substantive law.

The MBE's fundamental objective is to measure fairly, and efficiently which law school graduates have the necessary academic qualifications to be admitted to the bar and exceed this threshold.

The multiple-choice exam used to accomplish this objective must be of a consistent level of difficulty.

The level at which the pass decision is made must be achievable by most candidates.

The MBE tests the following skills:

- reading carefully and critically
- identifying the legal issue in a set of facts
- knowing the law that governs the legal issues tested
- distinguish between frequently confused closely-related principles
- making reasonable judgments from ambiguous facts
- understanding how limiting words make plausible-sounding choices wrong
- choosing the correct answer by intelligently eliminating incorrect choices

Notes for active learning

Preparation Strategies for the Bar Exam

An effective bar exam study plan

There are a lot of great ideas about how to prepare. Follow through with these ideas and turn them into persistent action for successful preparation.

A detailed and well-planned study schedule has benefits, such as giving you a sense of control and building confidence and proficiency.

Pick a date about 12-14 weeks before the exam (November for the February exam and April for the July exam) and use it as the start of your active study period.

Start a month earlier than many others to have a month to review as final preparation at the end.

Students have found this effective. Use an elongated prep period as a study schedule.

Most examinees prefer at least two weeks before the exam to review the material.

By planning early, you will have more time. You may want three or four final weeks to review subjects, take timed exams, and ensure that you are prepared to take the exam.

A few notes on schedule management:

> Do not *start* memorizing during your initial review period. You should be learning every week from the beginning of your study schedule. This final prep period is for reviewing and taking timed exams.

> If you stretch the study schedule over several months, plan review weeks into your schedule. For example, every four weeks, use a few days to review the governing law and take timed exams. This is a practical and fruitful approach as you will be more likely to retain the information.

Pick specific dates for specific tasks; this makes it more likely you will complete them.

Make sure the tasks are measurable. (e.g., practice two MEE essays).

Be realistic about the tasks, time, energy, and your ability to complete the items listed as tasks in preparation for the exam.

Remember to take some scheduled breaks from studying.

Exercise, sleep and take care of your physical and mental health.

If you are not in the right mental state preparing for the exam, you will likely be ineffective when studying and are less likely to pass the exam.

Focused studying

Some people are better at multiple-choice questions; others do better with essays.

The multiple-choice portion (MBE at 50%) and the essay portion (MEE at 30% and MPT at 20%) are weighted equally.

Doing poorly in one section means it will be challenging to achieve a passing score.

Identify weaknesses early in the preparation process and focus on them.

If you struggle with multiple-choice questions, dedicate extra time to practicing MBE questions.

If you struggle with writing, focus on completing MEE essays and complete MPT practice materials.

By reviewing your performance on released multiple-choice practice tests, be concerned if you consistently miss questions that are most answered correctly.

If you have problems with questions and perform below 50%, you lack the fundamental knowledge necessary to pass the MBE.

When reviewing your answers to practice questions, it is essential to review all questions and answers, even those you got right.

Make sure you got that correct answer for the right reason.

Reviewing the questions and answers is critical for success on the exam.

Spend time reviewing those basic principles and working deliberately on the straightforward (and easy) questions that supplement learning.

Advice on using outlines

As a user of this governing law book, several of the following points are moot. They are included, so you can be confident that you are using the proper resources to prep for the bar.

Having a useful governing law study guide (such as this book) is critical.

Without effective resources, it is challenging to understand, learn and apply the governing law to the facts given in the question.

Some students use outlines that make learning difficult.

A few common mistakes about outlines:

- Learning outlines that are too long (e.g., more than 100 pages per subject) or too short (e.g., a seven-page Contracts outline). You will be overwhelmed by information or never learn enough governing law.

- Spending too much time comparing several outlines for the same subject.

    For example, using different Contracts outlines and needlessly comparing them. This confusion results in an undue focus on insignificant discrepancies.

- Outlining every subject. If you are not starting to study early, this consumes too much study time. Do not attempt to outline all subjects. It may be a good idea to outline a select few problematic subjects.

Using a detailed and well-organized governing law outline (e.g., this book) is essential; it saves time, organizes concepts, reduces anxiety, and helps you score well and pass the bar.

Easy questions make the difference

Limitations on the examiners lead to the first important insight into preparation for the exam – the kind of questions that decide whether you pass.

Performance on specific questions correlates with success or failure on the bar.

By analyzing statistics, questions predicting success or failure have been identified.

In general, the most challenging questions were not particularly good predictors of failure because most people who missed them passed the bar.

However, many of the straightforward questions were excellent predictors of success.

The median raw score ranges from about 60% to 66% correct on the MBE.

The National Conference of Bar Examiners (NCBE) writes, "expert panelists reported that they believed MBE items were generally easy, correctly estimating that about 66% of candidates would select the right answer to a typical item."

Depending on the exam's difficulty, in most states, scoring slightly below the median (miss up to 80 questions) still passes.

The most important questions to determine if you pass are not the exceedingly challenging ones but the easy ones where 90% of the examinees answer correctly.

The easy questions usually test a basic and regularly tested point of substantive law.

The wrong choices (i.e., the distracters) are typically easy to eliminate.

Your first task in preparing for the MBE is to get easy questions correct.

Study plan based upon statistics

These statistics show that an excellent performance on either the MBE questions (approximately 67% correct) or the state essays (4s on essays) assures you a passing score.

If you fail the MBE by 9 points or the essays by 5 points, the probability of passing the bar is in the single digits.

Put effort into performing well on the MBE questions for the following reasons.

- The questions are objective, and there are enough questions that are predictable concerning content and structure that it is possible, through reasonable effort, to answer 67% of the questions correctly.

- Studying the MBE first has the added advantage of preparing the necessary substantive law for state essays.

- The essays cover several subjects, the precise topic tested is unpredictable, and the answers are graded subjectively by graders who work quickly.

You had three years of law school practice with essays and less experience with multiple-choice questions.

Master the MBE before spending time preparing for the essays.

Factors associated with passing the bar

Based on an analysis of statistics from students' performance, the following factors predict the likelihood of passing the bar:

LSAT score

First-year Grade Point Average (GPA)

LSAT scores are a significant predictor of success on the bar because the LSAT requires similar multiple-choice test-taking skills as the MBE.

The LSAT tests many of the types of legal reasoning tested on the MBE.

A lower LSAT can be overcome by a comprehensive study of the MBE governing law, but these students must work harder.

Most of the subjects tested (e.g., constitutional law, civil procedure, contracts, criminal law, real property, torts) on the MBE are taken in the first year of law school.

First-year GPA measures mastery of subjects, preparedness for exams, and the ability to understand legal principles and apply them to given fact patterns.

The MBE measures the same factors but in a multiple-choice format instead of essays.

Pass rates based on GPA and LSAT scores

Past statistics indicate that law students with LSAT scores above 155 and a first-year GPA above 3.0 are reasonably assured of passing the bar.

They should study conscientiously and take practice MBEs to perform at the level needed, but they have little cause to panic.

Students with LSAT scores between 150 and 155 and a first-year GPA between 2.5 and 3.0 are in a bit more danger of failing and need to undertake rigorous preparation.

They must achieve a scaled score of 135 and take released practice exams and understand the reasons for incorrect choices. They should prepare for state essays by learning the governing laws in this book.

Students with LSAT scores between 145 and 150 and a first-year GPA between 2.2 and 2.5 have a moderate chance of passing the bar from deliberate efforts.

These students should not rely on ordinary commercial bar reviews and need intense training, particularly on the MBE component of the bar. They must devote 50-60 hours per week for seven weeks to prepare for the bar by learning the format and content of substantive law tested on the MBE. They should take released practice exams under exam conditions and conscientiously study the questions missed.

Students with LSAT scores below 145 and a GPA below 2.2 have had a failure rate of approximately 80%.

They must prep faithfully and conscientiously beyond the advice above and must engage in a rigorous course of study, more than is demanded by a traditional bar review course.

Notes for active learning

Learning and Applying the Substantive Law

Knowledge of substantive law

The fundamental reason for missing a question is 1) a failure to know the principle of law controlling the answer or 2) failure to understand how that principle is applied.

You must know and apply the governing law to pass the bar. If you do not know the governing law, you will not apply it to answer correctly.

Many students *think* they understand the governing law but do not know the nuances. Do not assume that you understand the governing (i.e., substantive) law. It is prevalent for students not to know the governing law well.

Re-learn the substantive and procedural law taught in first-year courses.

A major mistake is not to memorize the governing law outlined in this book.

The multiple-choice and essay portions test nuances and details of governing law. It is essential to analyze the governing law as it is applied in the context of the question.

On the multiple-choice section, many questions require fine-line distinctions between similar principles of law.

Several multiple-choice answers will *seem* correct, given the limited time to answer. If your knowledge of the governing law is suboptimal, you will not make these subtle distinctions and will have to guess on many questions.

For the essay to be developed, you must know the governing law and apply it to the issues within the call of the question.

If you do not know the governing law, you will not state the correct rule in your essay. You will be unable to apply the correct rule to the fact pattern.

Where to find the law

The questions must be related to the subject matter outlined in the bar examiners' (NCBE) materials.

While the NCBE outline is broad and ambiguous, years of experience with the exam delineate the scope of material you must learn.

The governing law covered in this book is foundational to the exam. The governing law statements were compiled by analyzing questions released by the multistate examiners. The analysis revealed a limited number of legal principles repeatedly tested.

Review these principles before taking practice exams and understand how they are applied to obtain the correct answer.

The property questions are probably the most difficult. The fact patterns are usually long and involve many parties in complex transactions.

In preparing for the exam, learn basic property principles and apply them. However, extensive studying into property law's crevices is not necessary to score well on these questions.

Feel confident that you do not have to go beyond the information provided in this book to find the governing law.

Controlling authority

The examiners have specified the sources of authority for the correct answers.

In Constitutional Law and Criminal Procedure, it is Supreme Court decisions.

In Criminal Law, it is common law.

In Evidence, the Federal Rules of Evidence controls.

In Torts and Property, it is the generally accepted view of United States law.

The UCC is the controlling authority in sales (Article 2) questions.

The NCBE released questions, and the published answers determine the controlling law through deduction.

Recent changes in the law

The exam is prepared months before it is given because of logistical requirements. Therefore, the examiners cannot incorporate recent changes in the law into the questions.

Recent changes in the law will not form the basis for correct answers.

If a recent change makes an answer initially designated as the correct answer to be incorrect, the examiners will credit more than one answer.

The recent holding of a Supreme Court case will not be tested for about two years since the decision was published.

Lesser-known issues and unusual applications

Some of the challenging exam questions are based on obscure principles of law.

Missing the most challenging questions will not cause you to fail the exam if you have a solid understanding of the governing law. You can learn these principles and answer the question correctly, thereby improving your overall performance.

There are instances where the correct answers are different from the usual rules.

For example, hearsay evidence inadmissible at trial is admissible before a judge hearing evidence on a preliminary question of fact (e.g., Federal Rules of Evidence 104(a)).

Practice applying the governing law

Some students know the governing law but have problems *applying* it to the facts.

The exam is as much about testing skills as it is about testing the governing law.

Therefore, knowledge of the governing law is not enough to pass.

You must practice answering multiple-choice questions and writing well-organized, coherent, and complete essays where you apply the governing law to the given facts.

Know which governing law is being tested

A typical wrong answer (i.e., distracter) on a question is an answer which is correct under a body of law other than the governing law being tested.

An example is a question governed by Article 2 of the Uniform Commercial Code (UCC), where an offer is irrevocable if:

1) it is in writing,

2) made by a merchant, and

3) states that it is irrevocable.

One of the wrong answers states the correct rule under the common law of contracts, where an offer is revocable unless consideration is paid (i.e., an option) for the promise to keep it open.

Answers which are always wrong

Some commonly used distracters are always wrong and can be eliminated quickly.

For example, a choice in an evidence question says, "character can only be attacked by reputation evidence." This choice is wrong because both opinion and reputation evidence is admissible under the Federal Rules of Evidence when character attacks are permissible.

Honing Reading Skills

Reading skills are critical. The basic level is reading to understand the facts, identify the issue and keep the parties distinct. A mistake at this juncture results in answering incorrectly, no matter how much law is known.

Understanding complex transactions

If the question involves a transaction with many parties, diagram the transaction before analyzing the choices.

The diagram should show the relationship between the parties (e.g., grantor-grantee, assignor-assignee), the transaction date, and the person's relationships in the transaction (e.g., donee, *bona fide* purchaser).

Impediments to careful reading

Two reasons candidates fail to read carefully are:

1) hurrying through a question,

2) fatigue due to a lack of sleep or strain caused by the exam.

A careful test taker maintains a steady, deliberate pace during the exam. Practice in advance and be well-rested on the test day.

Reading too much into a question

The examiners are committed to designing questions, which are "a fair index of whether the applicant has the ability to practice law." Psychometric experts ensure that they are fair and unbiased.

Even though you must read every word of these carefully drafted questions, do not read the question to find some bizarre interpretation.

The examiners must ask fair questions and not rely on "tricks." Reading too much into a question and looking for a trick lurking behind every fact leads to the wrong answer often.

It is the straightforward questions that determine whether you pass, not the occasional challenging question that tests some arcane principle of law.

Therefore, take questions at face value.

Read the call of the question first

Before reading the facts, read the call of the question because it indicates the task for selecting the correct answer. This perspective focuses your attention before reading the facts.

The question contains many *words of art*, such as "most likely," "best defense," or "least likely," which govern the correct answer.

The call is often phrased positively; the "best argument" or "most likely result."

Read answers for consistency with the question and eliminate inconsistent choices.

Negative calls

When the call of the question is negative, asking for the "weakest argument" or asking which of the options is "not" in a specified category, examine each option with the perspective that the choice with those negative characteristics is the correct answer.

After reading and understanding the question stem, read the call of the question again before reading the choices.

Analyze each choice with the requirements specified in the call of the question.

Read all choices

Never pick an answer until carefully reading all the choices. The objective is to pick the best answer, which cannot be determined until comparing the choices.

Sometimes the difference between the right and wrong answer is that one choice is more detailed or precisely sets forth the applicable law. You do not know that until reading all the answers carefully.

Broad statements of black letter law may be correct

When reading an answer, do not rule out choices with imprecise statements of the applicable *black letter* law.

If the examiners always included a choice that was precisely on point, the questions would be too easy. Instead, they often disguise the wording used in the correct answer.

For example, the Federal Rules of Evidence contain an elaborate set of relevancy rules that limit the right to introduce evidence of repairs after an accident. If there was a question where the introduction of that evidence was permissible, and no choices specifically cite the exception to the general rule of exclusion, an answer phrased with the general rule of relevancy "Admissible because its probative value outweighs its prejudicial effect," would be the correct answer.

Multiple-Choice Test-Taking Tactics

Determine the single correct answer

Increase the odds of picking the correct answer based on technical factors independent of substantive (governing) law knowledge.

The examiners' limitation is that every question must have one demonstrably correct and three demonstrably incorrect answers, limiting how the examiners write the choices.

From the question's construction, this limitation may give clues about the answer.

Process of elimination

Answering a multiple-choice question is not finding the ideal answer to the question asked but instead picking the best option.

Eliminate choices and evaluate the remaining choice for plausibility.

Eliminate choices that state an incorrect proposition of law or do not relate to the facts.

If you eliminate three options and the remaining one is acceptable, pick it and move on.

Elimination increases the odds

It takes about 125 correct answers to pass the MBE. An important strategy in reaching that number is intelligently eliminating choices.

If you are sure of the answer to only 50 of the 200 questions on the exam and confidently eliminate two of the four choices on the remaining 150 questions. Guess between the two remaining choices, and the odds predict 75 correct.

Those 75 correct, coupled with 50 questions you were confident of the answer, produce a raw score of 125 on the MBE and a scaled score above the benchmark 135.

Unfortunately, you cannot avoid guessing on questions, but intelligent methods reduce options to only two viable choices.

Sometimes you might not be able to eliminate the wrong answers just because you are sure of the answer to one of the choices. Eliminating with confidence even one choice increases the probability of correctly answering the question.

Eliminating two wrong answers

Specific questions on the MBE are challenging because of distinguishing between two choices when selecting the best answer.

A typical comment from examinees leaving the exam is, "I could not decide between the last two choices."

The positive side of that problem is eliminating two of the four choices.

Pick the winning side

The most common choice pattern is the "two-two" pattern – two choices state that the plaintiff prevails, and two that the defendant prevails.

The best approach for this type of question is to rely on your knowledge of the law or instinctive feeling to which conclusion is correct.

In a question with two choices on one side and two on the other side of a court's decision, first, pick a choice on the side you think should prevail.

Distinguish between the explanations following this conclusion and pick the choice that best justifies it.

Distance between choices on the other side

If the justifications following the conclusion for the side you chose seem indistinguishable, look at the explanations for the choices on the other side.

If the reasons for the choices on the other side are readily distinguishable, and one appears reasonable and the other incorrect, reconsider your initial conclusion.

Remember, the examiner is required to provide a distinguishable reason why one explanation of a general conclusion is correct, and the other is wrong.

That obligation does not exist if the general conclusion itself is incorrect.

Suppose choices (A) and (B) on one side look correct; that is, they are reasonable and consistent with the fact pattern. One of the choices with the opposite conclusion, answer (C), seems incorrect or inconsistent with the facts, and answer (D) with the same general conclusion sounds reasonable. From a strictly technical viewpoint, the best choice is answer (D).

Questions based upon a common fact pattern

There are several instances where two or more questions are based on the same facts.

Look at the second question's wording to guide the first question's correct answer. When asked to assume an answer to a first question from a fact pattern to answer the second question, the probability is high that the answer to the first question follows that assumption.

For example, if the first question has two choices beginning with "P prevails" and two with "D prevails," and the second question starts with "If P prevails," it is likely one of the "P prevails" choices is correct for the first question. If you picked "D prevails," think carefully before selecting it as the final answer.

Multiple true/false issues

In addition to true/false questions, the exam sometimes states three propositions in the root of the question and tests characteristics of those propositions in the call of the question.

The choices list various combinations of propositions.

The difference between this type of question and the double true/false question is that only four of the eight possible combinations fit into the options. It is possible to answer correctly even if you are not sure of all propositions' truth or falsity but are sure of one.

Correctly stated, but the inapplicable principle of law

The task of the examiners is to make the wrong choices look attractive. A creative way to accomplish this is to write a choice that impeccably states a rule of law that is not applicable because of facts in the root of the question.

For example, in a question where a person is an assignee, not a sublessee, one of the choices may correctly state the law for sublessees, but it is inapplicable to the fact pattern.

Therefore, these answer choices with inapplicable law can be confidently eliminated.

"Because" questions

Conjunctions are commonly used in the answers. It is essential to understand their role in determining whether a choice is correct.

The word "because" connects a conclusion and the reason for that conclusion with the facts in the body of the question.

There are two requirements for a question using "because" to be correct:

1) the conclusion must be correct,

2) the reasoning must logically follow based upon facts in the question, and the statement which follows "because" must be legally correct.

If the "because" choice has the correct result for the wrong reason, it is incorrect.

"If" questions

The conjunction "if" requires a much narrower focus than "because."

When a choice contains an "if," determine whether the entire statement is true, assuming that the proposition which follows the "if" is true.

There is no requirement that facts in the root of the question support the proposition following "if." There is no requirement for facts in the question to support the proposition that such a construction be reasonable.

"Because" or "if" need not be exclusive

There is no requirement for the conclusion following "if" or "because" to be exclusive.

For example, if a master could be liable in tort under the doctrine of *respondeat superior* or because the master was *negligent*, a choice using "if" or "because" holding the master liable would be correct if it stated either reason, even though the master might be liable for the other reason.

Exam tip for "because"

Notice that in an answer that would have been correct, the word "because" limits the facts you could consider to those in the body of the question containing specific facts.

The difference between the effect of "if" and "because" controls the answer.

Identify those limited situations (e.g., where the appropriate standard is strict liability) and distinguish them from those that are satisfactory (e.g., if the standard is negligence).

"Only if" requires exclusivity

Sometimes the words "only if" are used to distinguish between the two "affirmed" choices to make one wrong.

When an option uses the words "only if," assume that the entire proposition is correct as long as the words following "only if" are true.

The critical difference, where "only if" is used, is that the proposition cannot be true except when the condition is true. If there is another reason for the same result to be reached, the choice is wrong.

"Unless" questions

The conjunction "unless" has the same function as "only if," except that it precedes a negative exclusive condition instead of a positive exclusive condition.

It is essentially the mirror image of an "only if" choice.

For an option using "unless," reverse and substitute the words "only if" for "unless."

Limiting words

Choices can be made incorrect with limiting words that require that a proposition be true in all circumstances or under no circumstances.

Examples of limiting words include *all*, *any*, *never*, *always*, *only*, *every*, and *plenary*.

Notes for active learning

Making Correct Judgment Calls

Applying the law to the facts

Most questions give a fact pattern and ask which choice draws the correct legal conclusion required by the call of the question.

The first skill required is to draw inferences from facts given to place the conduct described in the question in the appropriate legal category.

The second skill is to apply the appropriate legal rule to conduct in that category and choose the option which reaches the appropriate conclusion.

The process of drawing inferences from a fact pattern and placing conduct in an appropriate category often requires judgment.

Bad judgment equals the wrong answer

To make the questions difficult, the examiners often place the conduct near the border of two different legal classifications.

Decide which side of the demarcation the conduct falls on. Inevitably, reasonable people can differ on these judgments.

If your judgment does not match the examiners, you will likely answer the question incorrectly, no matter how much law you know.

Mitigate this problem by reviewing released questions involving judgment calls where the examiners have published correct answers (i.e., their judgment call).

For example, a death occurring because the parties played Russian roulette is considered *depraved heart murder*, not *involuntary manslaughter*.

Judgment calls happen

Difficult judgment calls occur several times on the exam, and you are likely to make some close judgment calls incorrectly.

While this adds to the frustrations of multiple-choice tests, it is part of the exam.

By narrowing judgment call questions to two choices and guessing, you will get approximately half of them correct.

You will not fail the exam solely because you were unlucky on judgment calls.

The examiners remove many judgment calls by procedural devices.

The importance of procedure

The question may not ask what a jury should find on the facts.

The answer may be controlled by the procedural context of the criminal prosecution.

For example, it is given that the jury has found the defendant guilty of murder, and the only question on appeal is whether the judge should have granted a motion to dismiss at the end of hearing evidence. This is because a reasonable jury looking at the facts and inferences most favorable to the prosecution should not have found the defendant guilty of murder.

The same procedural issues exist when the question asks if a motion for summary judgment should be allowed or if the court should direct a verdict.

Exam Tips and Suggestions

Timing is everything

The time given to complete the exam is usually adequate if you practiced enough questions to improve speed and efficiency to the required level.

As you get closer to the test date, just doing practice questions is not enough.

You need to time your practice. Take previously released exams in two three-hour periods on the same day. Since these practice exams are approximately the same length as the exam, you will know if you have a timing problem.

If you do not practice under timed conditions, you risk exhausting time on the exam before answering all the questions.

Practice your timing under test-like conditions to know if the timing will be an issue. If you cannot complete the practice exam, you will have trouble with the exam.

If time is an issue, adjust your pace and continue practicing.

All questions do not require the same amount of time.

An approach for when time is not an issue

If you can complete 100 questions in three hours, use this strategy. At the start of the exam, break the allotted time into 15-minute intervals and write them down.

Set an initial pace of 9 questions every fifteen minutes.

Check your progress at each 15-minute interval.

If you completed 18 questions in the first half-hour, 36 in the first hour, 72 in the first two hours, and 90 in the first two and a half hours, you are on target to complete the exam on time. At this pace, you should complete 100 questions in two hours and forty-six minutes.

This leaves 14 minutes to check the answer sheet, revisit troublesome questions, or use the time to go a little slower on the last questions when fatigue impairs acuity.

If you find that your careful pace is faster than the budgeted 9 questions every 15 minutes, work at a faster pace, but use the extra time on the more challenging questions or in rechecking your work at the end.

Do *not* change the original answer choice unless you have a specific reason.

It is unwise to leave the exam early.

An approach for when time is an issue

During practice, continue answering questions to complete the section even after the time for self-paced exams has expired. Note which question you completed within the allocated time. Strive to complete the questions within the allotted time during your final exam prep.

If you learn from taking the practice test that you may not finish the questions in the allotted time on the actual exam, skip those questions with a long fact pattern followed by only one question. Keep your place on the answer sheet by skipping the row.

Return to those questions at the end and complete as many as time permits. Before turning your exam in, guess at the rest to reduce the number of random guesses.

Answer every question, even if you have not read the question, since wrong answers do *not* count against you.

Difficult questions

If you do not know the answer, do not spend a disproportionate amount of time on it since each question counts the same. Mark it in the test booklet, make a shrewd guess within the budgeted time and come back if time allows.

Do *not* leave questions unanswered. No points are deducted for wrong answers.

Minimize fatigue to maximize your score

The mental energy required to answer all the multiple-choice questions under stress produces fatigue (even with a lunch break).

Fatigue slows processing questions effectively and impairs reading comprehension. You may process questions more slowly at the end of each session and more quickly at the beginning before fatigue sets in.

Take at least two released exams under timed conditions to know how significantly fatigue affects your performance.

Be sure to arrive at the exam site on time. If necessary, stay at a nearby hotel rather than getting up early and risking a long drive the morning of the exam.

Relax during the lunch break and do not discuss the morning session with others.

You should know enough about your metabolism to eat the correct foods during the exam and reinforce appropriate caffeine levels if appropriate.

Proofread the answer sheet

As you decide on each correct answer, circle the corresponding letter in the exam book, and mark the appropriate block on the answer sheet.

The answer sheet is the only document graded by the examiners.

At the pace of 9 questions per 15 minutes, about 14 minutes should remain. Spend that time proofreading the answer sheet. Verify the answers circled to be certain that you marked the appropriate block on the answers.

Ensure that there are no blanks, and no questions have two answers.

Do *not* use this time to change an answer already selected unless you have a particularly good reason to change it.

If you have erased, ensure the erasure is thorough, or the computer may reject the answer because it cannot distinguish between marked answers.

If you have time after proofreading, review the problematic questions, and re-think the answers chosen. However, even after careful thought, hesitate to change an answer.

Do not leave any section of the exam early; use the allotted time wisely.

Intelligent preparation over a sustained period

There is no easy way to conquer an exam as challenging and comprehensive as the MBE, except through practice and an investment of time and effort well before the exam.

By diligently preparing, practicing questions, and intelligently assessing why questions were answered incorrectly, your skills for the exam will improve substantially.

Continue to improve those skills by following the advice given herein until reaching a proficiency level enabling you to pass the bar. This proficiency is accurately measured in multiple-choice format questions.

Some students will have to work harder to achieve the required proficiency.

The tools are in this study guide, and any law school graduate can be successful in passing the bar if they invest the required time and effort to be prepared.

Notes for active learning

Essay Preparation Strategies and Essay-Writing Suggestions

Memorize the law

Do not make the mistake of waiting too long before memorizing the governing law. Start learning the governing law early to be better prepared and pass the exam.

Memorize essential principles and focus on highly tested governing law.

Focus on the highly tested essay rules

Do not treat all subjects the same when you prepare for the essay portion of the exam.

Some governing law topics are tested more than others. It is crucial to focus on the highly tested topics (e.g., torts, contracts. property, civil procedure).

Know and apply enough governing laws to pass the bar – focus on commonly tested governing laws (e.g., negligence) provided in this book.

Practice writing essay answers each week

Practicing is crucial to a high score on essays. Practice regularly and avoid procrastination for this essential component of bar prep.

Incorporate practicing essay writing into your exam study schedule. To reduce procrastination, schedule time for writing practice essays each week.

For the MPT, practice by drafting full MPTs. Most examinees procrastinate on preparing for the MPT; there is nothing to memorize.

Do not make the *fatal mistake* of not practicing. The MPT portion is worth 20% of the UBE score.

Know the format and *practice that format to* increase your UBE score. This practice will increase your score and the probability of passing the bar.

Add one essay-specific subject each week

The Multistate Essay Exam (MEE) subjects include the 7 MBE subjects plus the 5 subjects of Business Associations (Agency, Partnerships, Corporations, and LLCs), Conflict of Laws, Family Law, Trusts and Estates, and Secured Transactions (UCC Article 9).

Combine highly tested subjects (e.g., torts) with less-tested subjects (e.g., secured transactions) and complex topics (e.g., contracts) with easier topics (e.g., business associations).

From preparation, know which subjects you struggle with and require a focused effort to master the essential governing law.

Make it easy for the grader to award points

Your answer to a question will probably be read in less than five minutes by a grader with a checklist to find that you have seen the issues and discussed them intelligently. Writing organized and clear answers makes it easy for the essay grader to award points.

Use headings for each of the major issues.

If the question suggests a structure for the answer because it is divided into parts or because the facts present a series of discrete issues, use the structure of the question, which is probably the structure of the checklist.

Use the IRAC method for the essay questions: state the issue, state the Rule. Apply the rule to the facts and conclude. IRAC seems simple, but following this approach makes it easier for the grader to know that you identified and addressed every issue and applied the law to the facts given.

IRAC results in more points during the exam.

Do not spend time trying to formulate eloquent issue statements. The question often outlines the issues, so an eloquent issue statement is redundant, and issue statements do not earn extra points.

Many examinees spend too much time developing an impressive issue statement and omit other essentials of their analysis (e.g., truncated analysis section).

An issue statement "Torts" or "Is the defendant liable for negligence?" is enough.

Do not waste time arguing both sides. There are no "two sides" for many essays to argue on bar essays because these are not law school essays.

Apply the law to facts and conclude unless asserting each party has good arguments.

Conclusion for each essay question

Points will be lost unless you conclude for each issue identified in the facts or are asked to address it in the call of the question.

Use caution starting the essay with the conclusion unless confident it is correct.

Many sample answers provided by the National Conference of Bar Examiners start with a definite and strong conclusion. Use caution to start with a conclusion unless confident (e.g., NCBE sample responses) your conclusion is correct.

Starting with a conclusion that is not correct draws attention to an incorrect conclusion at the start, which may influence the grader disproportionality. The grader may lose faith in your answer from the onset, and it is advisable to have a neutral heading rather than a firm conclusion that is wrong.

Tips for an easy-to-read essay

Use paragraph breaks between the Issue, Rule, Analysis, and Conclusion. Paragraph break makes it easy for the grader to read and score your essays. Additionally, this approach makes the answer appear longer and more complete.

Emphasize keywords and phrases. Underline key phrases so the grader notices that you addressed the governing law and applied it to the facts given.

After graders score several essays on the same topic, they scan essays for specific phrases that they expect to locate within a complete essay.

Think before you write

Read each question carefully to understand the facts and their necessary implications thoroughly and accurately.

After skimming the question, spend time on the focus line at the end of the question. Review the facts with the call of the question in mental focus.

Write a short outline of the issues raised. Outline in your mind the issues; state to yourself the tentative conclusions; test each conclusion from the standpoints of law and common sense; revise, as necessary.

Decide on a logical, orderly, and convincing arrangement for the response. Until then, you are not ready to write the answer.

Of the thirty-six minutes allotted to each essay, spend 15 minutes on issue spotting and organization and about twenty minutes writing the answer.

The ability to think and communicate like a lawyer

The Board knows that you have completed law school, under competent instructors, and have passed law school exams. The bar does not challenge the results of your law school courses.

The exam tests the ability to apply what you have learned to facts that might arise in practice and which, in some instances, involve several fields of law. The value of an answer depends not only on the correctness of the conclusions but on displaying essential legal principles and thinking like a lawyer.

Conclude on each issue presented. If a conclusion is derived from fuzzy facts, construct a well-reasoned argument supporting your conclusion to receive full credit regardless of if you conclude the same as the examiners.

If the correct answer depends on a provision of substantive law, which you are not familiar with, you can obtain a passing answer to the question by reaching a well-reasoned conclusion applying general law principles.

Do not try to limit the question to a particular subject area. Many questions combine traditional subjects, and you must be prepared to answer the question applying principles you learned across various subjects.

Do not restate the facts

The examiners know the facts; there is no time to waste. Do not restate the facts but use them to apply and integrate legal principles in writing the essay.

Do not fight the facts, particularly the focus line of the question.

For example, if the facts state that A executed a valid will, write about valid wills. If the question asks you to argue on behalf of A, do not argue on behalf of B because B has a prevailing argument. However, raise potential arguments which could be made on behalf of B and counter them in arguing on behalf of A.

Do not state abstract or irrelevant propositions of law

It is usually undesirable to begin an answer with a legal proposition. If the proposition is applicable, it will be more appropriate later to indicate the reason for your conclusion. If it is not applicable, do not state a surplus fact or legal principle.

Although it is seldom necessary to state an applicable rule of law in detail, make a sufficient reference to it so that the examiner appreciates your knowledge of the principle and conditions when it applies.

Do not, by speculating on different facts, nor in other ways, work into your answer some point of law with which you happen to be familiar, but which does not apply to the answer. Importantly, the examiners are not interested in knowing how many rules of law you know, but your ability to apply the applicable rules to the facts.

If the question says that A and B in the above hypothetical are unrelated, do not talk about the results which would occur if they were husband and wife.

Use the principles of law applicable to the call of the question and the facts. You must state the principles of applicable law to demonstrate to the examiner that you know the elements of the rule and how they apply to these facts.

For example, if the facts said that A transferred to B (a non-relative) the money necessary for B to purchase Blackacre from C and asks who owns Blackacre, you would say, "Since A furnished the consideration for the purchase of Blackacre and B took the title to the property in their name, B holds title to Blackacre in a resulting trust for A.

Do not detail the black letter law of resulting trusts since you have shown your knowledge by properly applying the facts to the law of resulting trusts.

Do not fight the facts and address a contrary fact not presented. The examiners may take points away if you make that mistake because you are not focused on the issues presented.

Discuss all the issues raised

A grasp of all the issues is essential.

For example, if there are three issues in a question, a discussion of only one issue, no matter how masterly, if coupled with omitting the others, could not result in 100% credit. It would probably result in a score of 33%.

The exam includes many issues in most questions so it can be graded mechanically. This maintains consistency across a group of several graders for each exam question.

The grader has a checklist of issues and awards most points for the examinee that identifies issues and intelligently discusses each.

Failure to see and discuss enough issues intelligently is probably the biggest reason for failure on the essay portion of the exam.

Methods for finding all issues

Use all the facts presented. Failure to discuss facts probably means that you missed important issues.

If you must decide in the early part of the question (e.g., does the court have jurisdiction) and you decide that issue so the remaining facts become irrelevant, make an alternative assumption ("If the court does have jurisdiction") and answer the question in the alternative using facts which would otherwise be irrelevant.

Do not avoid issues because you are not sure of the substantive law. If the examiners stated that X's nephew helped X escape after a crime, discuss the nephew's status as an accessory after the fact. If you do not know whether he is a close enough relative to be exempt under the statute, answer this issue by making alternative assumptions.

Indicators requiring alternative arguments

Ambiguous terms – if there are words in the fact pattern that are neutral or ambiguous such as "put up," the examiners look for possible interpretations of these terms.

Language in quotes – language placed in quotes is almost always ambiguous and must be construed as part of the answer.

Avoid ambiguous, rambling statements and verbosity

Generally, do not use compound sentences. Two separate sentences are preferred.

Complex sentences are particularly useful to apply the facts of the question to the applicable principle of law.

For example, in the previous resulting trust hypothetical, write, "Since B purchased Blackacre and took title in their name with money furnished by A, A holds title to Blackacre in a resulting trust, even if B has not signed a memorandum."

Avoid undue repetition

If the same principle of law and conclusion apply to two parts of an answer, state it once in detail, and refer back for the second part.

For example, if you have discussed A's liability and now must discuss B's liability, say, "B is also guilty of murder for the same reasons as A. (see discussion above)."

Avoid slang and colloquialism

The examiners judge your formal writing style.

If the examiner shows humor with names and events, do not show your sense of humor.

> Use the standard abbreviations:
>
> P for Plaintiff
>
> D for Defendant
>
> K for Contract
>
> BFP for *Bona Fide* purchaser

Write legibly and coherently

Printing is usually easier to read than handwriting.

Use all the pages, and do not crowd your answer.

Plan your answer so that you do not have to use inserts and arrows.

Timing strategies

On the MEE, you must complete six equally weighted essay questions in three hours; an average of 30 minutes per question.

You have flexibility with time limitations as questions are not of the same difficulty.

There are two absolute figures:

>spend no more than 45 minutes on any question,

>spend at least 20 minutes on each question.

Be careful about not going over the time limit on the first question because this will require a readjustment of your timing for the entire session. If you miss the deadlines, re-divide your remaining time so that you will have an equal amount of time on each question.

If you go over by 15 minutes a question, do not allocate 30 minutes for other questions.

Stay focused

Do not start by reading the entire exam. Answer the questions in order and do not consider more than one question at a time.

After answering, put it out of your mind and not worry about your response. Keep your mind clear to focus on the next question.

Proofread your answers as time permits.

Law school essay grading matrix

An "A" answer is an outstanding response. It correctly and fully identifies dispositive issues and sub-issues raised by the question. The answer states the applicable legal rules and sub-rules with precision. It analyzes the question thoroughly with the applicable rules and explores alternative analysis where appropriate. It applies the law to the facts to conclude and is not cluttered by irrelevant matters. An "A" answer demonstrates an objectively superior mastering of the subject. An answer is not an "A" answer simply because it is better than most students' answers.

A "B" answer is a good response. It presents the four components of a good answer (issues, rules, analysis & application, and conclusion), but it does so in a way that could be improved. For example, it may be that not all critical issues have been spotted, or the issues are not presented clearly. The statement of legal rules captures that basic law but may not develop the law's complexities or nuances. The analysis is competent but lacks subtlety and may be somewhat simplistic or conclusory.

A "C" answer is a minimally competent response. It contains the four components of a good answer (issues, rules, analysis & application, and conclusion) but may not distinguish them. Perhaps only some issues have been identified while others are missed. The rules of law lack completeness or accuracy. The analysis and application may be shallow and conclusory. Conclusions may be questionable and not well-defended.

A "D" answer lacks basic components. It may identify the wrong issues or none. Rules are stated incorrectly. The analysis is conclusory or absent. The law is not applied to the facts coherently. Conclusions are unsupported or missing. The response exhibits a lack of knowledge of legal issues and rules or demonstrates an inability to engage in legal analysis.

Best wishes with your preparation!

Appendix

Overview of American Law

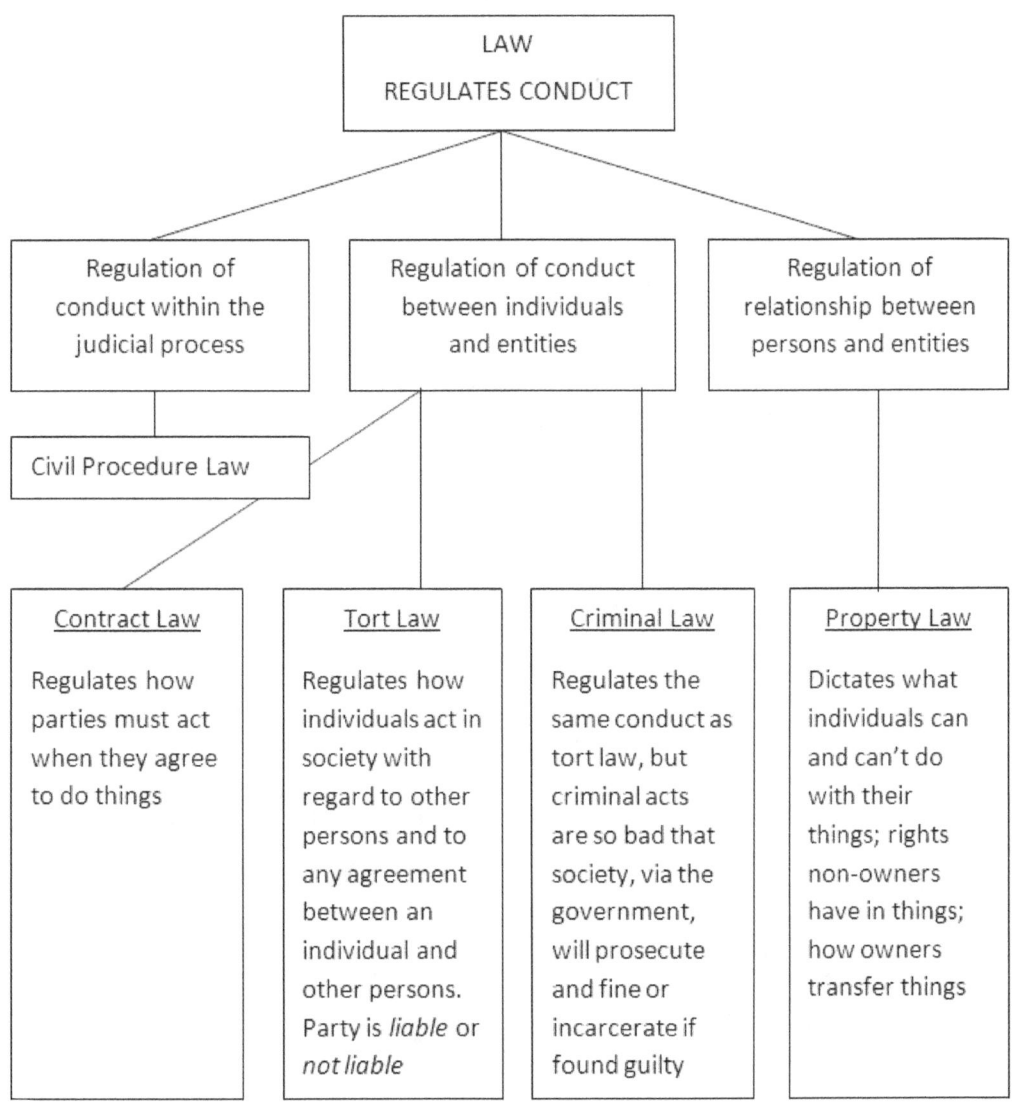

U.S. Court Systems – Federal and State Courts

There are two kinds of courts in the USA – federal courts and state courts.

Federal courts are established under the U.S. Constitution by Congress to decide disputes involving the Constitution and laws passed by Congress. A state establishes state and local courts (within states, local courts are established by cities, counties, and other municipalities).

Jurisdiction of federal and state courts

The differences between federal courts and state courts are defined by jurisdiction.[1] Jurisdiction refers to the kinds of cases that a particular court is authorized to hear and adjudicate (i.e., the pronouncement of a legally binding judgment upon the parties to the dispute).

Federal court jurisdiction is limited to the types of cases listed in the Constitution and specifically provided by Congress. For the most part, federal courts only hear:

- cases in which the United States is a party[2];
- cases involving violations of the U.S. Constitution or federal laws (under federal-question jurisdiction[3]);
- cases between citizens of different states if the amount in controversy *exceeds* $75,000 (under diversity jurisdiction[4]); and
- bankruptcy, copyright, patent, and maritime law cases.

State courts, in contrast, have broad jurisdiction, so the cases individual citizens are likely to be involved in (e.g., robberies, traffic violations, contracts, and family disputes) are usually heard and decided in state courts. The only cases state courts are not allowed to hear are lawsuits against the United States and those involving certain specific federal laws: criminal, antitrust, bankruptcy, patent, copyright, and some maritime law cases.

In many cases, both federal and state courts have jurisdiction whereby the plaintiff (i.e., the party initiating the suit) can choose whether to file their claim in state or federal court.

Criminal cases involving federal laws can be tried only in federal court, but most criminal cases involve violations of state law and are tried in state court. Robbery is a crime, but what law makes it is a crime? Except for certain exceptions, state laws, not federal laws, make robbery a crime. There are only a few federal laws about robbery, such as the law that makes it a federal crime to rob a bank whose deposits are insured by a federal agency. Examples of other federal crimes are the transport of illegal drugs into the country or across state lines and using the U.S. mail system to defraud consumers.

Crimes committed on federal property (e.g., national parks or military reservations) are prosecuted in federal court.

Federal courts may hear cases concerning state laws if the issue is whether the state law violates the federal Constitution. Suppose a state law forbids slaughtering animals outside of certain limited areas. A neighborhood association brings a case in state court against a defendant who sacrifices chickens in their backyard. When the court issues an order (i.e., an injunction[5]) forbidding the defendant from further sacrifices, the defendant challenges the state law in federal court as an unconstitutional infringement of religious freedom.

Some conduct is illegal under both federal and state laws. For example, federal laws prohibit employment discrimination, and the states have added additional legal restrictions. A person can file their claim in either federal or state court under federal law or federal and state laws. A case that only involves a state law can be brought only in state court.

Appeals for review of actions by federal administrative agencies are federal civil cases.

For example, if the Environmental Protection Agency, over the objection of area residents, issued a permit to a paper mill to discharge water used in its milling process into the Scenic River, the residents may appeal and have the federal court of appeals review the agency's decision.

---

[1] *jurisdiction* – 1) the legal authority of a court to hear and decide specific types of case; 2) the geographic area over which the court has the authority to decide cases.

[2] *parties* – the plaintiff and the defendant in a lawsuit.

[3] *federal-question jurisdiction* – the federal district courts' authorization to hear and decide cases arising under the Constitution, laws, or treaties of the United States.

[4] *diversity jurisdiction* – the federal district courts' authority to hear and decide civil cases involving plaintiffs and defendants who are citizens of different states (or U.S. citizens and foreign nationals) and meet specific statutory requirements.

[5] *injunction* – a judge's order that a party takes or refrain from taking a particular action. An injunction may be preliminary until the outcome of a case is determined or permanent.

Organization of the federal courts

Congress has divided the country into 94 federal judicial districts, with each having a U.S. district court. The U.S. district courts are the federal trial courts -- where federal cases are tried, witnesses testify, and juries serve.

Each district has a U.S. bankruptcy court, which is part of the district court that administers the U.S. bankruptcy laws.

Congress uses state boundaries to help define the districts. Some districts cover an entire state, like Idaho. Other districts cover just part of a state, like the Northern District of California. Congress placed each of the ninety-four districts in one of twelve regional circuits whereby each circuit has a court of appeals. The losing party can petition the court of appeals to review the case to determine if the district judge applied the law correctly.

There is a U.S. Court of Appeals for the Federal Circuit, whose jurisdiction is defined by subject matter rather than geography. It hears appeals from certain courts and agencies, such as the U.S. Court of International Trade, the U.S. Court of Federal Claims, and the U.S. Patent and Trademark Office, and certain types of cases from the district courts (mainly lawsuits claiming that patents have been infringed).

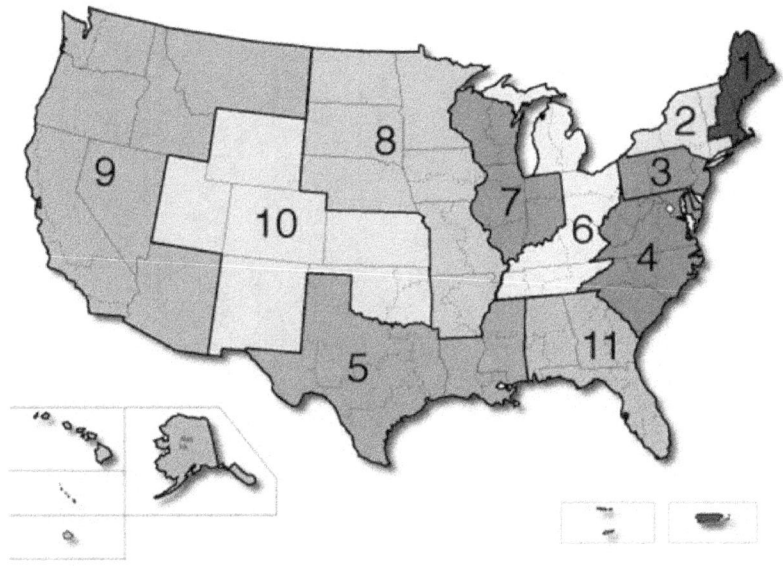

Twelve regional federal circuits

The Supreme Court in Washington, D.C., is the highest court in the nation. The losing party can petition in a case in the court of appeals (or, sometimes, in a state supreme court), can petition the Supreme Court to hear an appeal.

Unlike a court of appeals, the Supreme Court does not have to hear the case. The Supreme Court hears only a small percentage of the cases it is asked to review.

Notes for active learning

How Civil Cases Move Through the Federal Courts

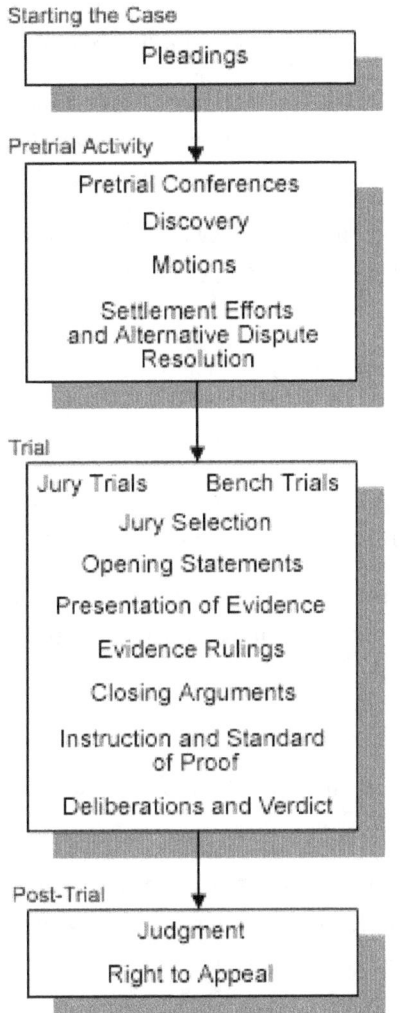

A federal civil case begins when a person, or their legal representative, files a paper with the clerk of the court that asserts another person's wrongful act injured the person. In legal terminology, the plaintiff files a *complaint* against the defendant.

The defendant files an *answer* to the complaint. These written statements of the party's positions are called pleadings. In some circumstances, the defendant may file a *motion* instead of an answer; the motion asks the court to take some action, such as dismiss the case or require the plaintiff to explain more clearly what the lawsuit is about.

Jury trials

In a jury trial, the jury decides what happened, and to apply the legal standards, the judge tells them to apply to reach a verdict. The plaintiff presents evidence supporting its view of the case, and the defendant presents evidence rebutting the plaintiff's evidence or supporting its view of the case. From these presentations, the jury must decide what happened and applied the law to those facts.

The jury never decides what law applies to the case; that is the role of the judge. For example, in a discrimination case where the plaintiff alleged that their workplace was hostile, the judge tells the jury the legal standard for a hostile environment.

The jury would have to decide whether the plaintiff's description of events was true and whether those events met the legal standard. A trial jury, or petit jury, may consist of six to twelve jurors in a civil case.

Bench trials

If the parties agree not to have a *jury trial* and leave the fact-finding to the judge, the trial is a *bench trial*. In bench and jury trials, the judge ensures the correct legal standards are followed.

In contrast to a jury trial, the judge decides the facts and renders the verdict in a *bench trial*.

For example, in a discrimination case in which the plaintiff alleged a hostile environment, the judge would determine the legal standard for a hostile environment and decide whether the plaintiff's description of events was true and whether those events met the legal standard.

Some kinds of cases always have bench trials. For example, there is never a jury trial if the plaintiff is seeking an injunction, an order from the judge that the defendant does, or stop doing something, as opposed to monetary damages.

Some statutes provide that a judge must decide the facts in certain types of cases.

Jury selection

A jury trial begins with the selection of jurors. Citizens are selected for jury service through a process set out in laws passed by Congress and in the federal rules of procedure.

First, citizens are called to court to be available to serve on juries. These citizens are selected at random from sources, in most districts, lists of registered voters, which may be augmented by other sources, such as lists of licensed drivers in the judicial district.

The judge and the lawyers choose who will serve on the jury.

To choose the jurors, the judge and sometimes the lawyers ask prospective jurors questions to determine if they will decide the case fairly, a process known as *voir dire*.

The lawyers may request that the judge excuse jurors they think may not be impartial, such as those who know a party in the case or who have had an experience that might make them favor one side over the other. These requests for rejecting jurors are *challenges for cause*.

The lawyers may request that the judge excuse a certain number of jurors without reason; these requests are *peremptory challenges*.

Instructions and standard of proof

Following the closing arguments, the judge gives instructions to the jury, explaining the relevant law, how the law applies to the case, and what questions the jury must decide.

How sure do jurors have to be before they reach a verdict? One important instruction the judge gives the jury is the standard of proof they must follow in deciding the case.

The courts, through their decisions, and Congress, through statutes, have established standards by which facts must be proven in criminal and civil cases.

In civil cases, to decide for the plaintiff, the jury must determine by a *preponderance of the evidence* that the defendant failed to perform a legal duty and violated the plaintiff's rights. A preponderance of the evidence means that, based on the evidence, the evidence favors the plaintiff more (even if only slightly) than it favors the defendant.

If the evidence in favor of the plaintiff could be placed on one side of a scale and that in favor of the defendant on the other, the plaintiff would win if the evidence in favor of the plaintiff was heavy enough to tip the scale. If the two sides were even, or if the scale tipped for the defendant, the defendant would win.

Judgment

In civil cases, if the jury (or judge) decides in favor of the plaintiff, the result usually is that the defendant must pay the plaintiff money or damages. The judge orders the defendant to pay the decided amount. Sometimes the defendant is ordered to take some specific action that will restore the plaintiff's rights. If the defendant wins the case, there is nothing more the trial court needs to do as the case is disposed of and the defendant is held not liable.

Right to appeal

The losing party in a federal civil case has a right to appeal the verdict to the U.S. court of appeals (i.e., Federal Circuit Courts) and ask the court to review the case to determine whether the trial was conducted properly. The losing party in the state trial court has a right to appeal the verdict to the state court of appeal.

The grounds for appeal usually are that the federal district (or state) judge made an error, either in the procedure (e.g., admitting improper evidence) or interpreting the law. The government may appeal in civil cases, as any other party may. Neither party may appeal if there was no trial -- parties settled their civil case out of court.

Notes for active learning

How Criminal Cases Move Through the Federal Courts

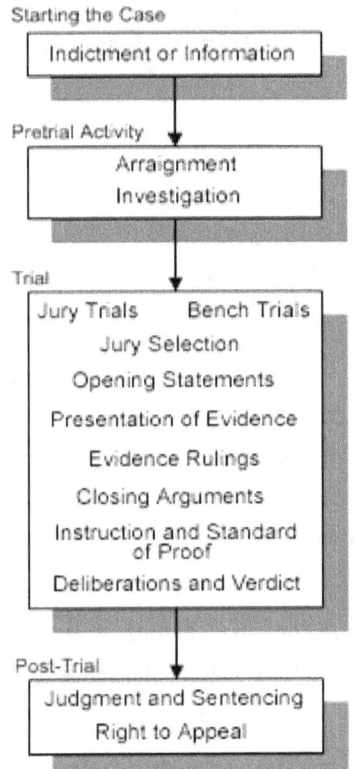

Indictment or information

A criminal case formally begins with an indictment or information, which is a formal accusation that a person committed a crime.

An indictment may be obtained when a lawyer (i.e., prosecutor) for the executive branch of the U.S. government (i.e., U.S. attorney or assistant U.S. attorney) present evidence to a federal grand jury that, according to the government, indicates a person committed a crime.

The U.S. attorney tries to convince the grand jury that there is enough evidence to show that the person probably committed the crime and should be formally accused. If the grand jury agrees, it issues an indictment.

A grand jury is different from a trial jury or petit jury.

A grand jury determines whether the person may be tried for a crime; a petit jury listens to the evidence presented at the trial and determines whether the defendant is guilty.

Petit is French for "small"; petit juries usually consist of twelve jurors in criminal cases.

Grand is French for "large"; grand juries have from sixteen to twenty-three jurors.

Grand jury indictments are most often used for *felonies* (i.e., punishable by imprisonment of more than a year or by death) such as bank robberies or sales of illegal drugs.

Grand jury indictments are not necessary to prosecute *misdemeanors* (i.e., less serious than a felony but more serious than an infraction) and are necessary for felonies.

For lesser crimes, the U.S. attorney issues an *information* that substitutes for an indictment. For example, speeding on a highway in a national park is a misdemeanor.

An information is used when a defendant waives an indictment by a grand jury.

Arraignment

After the grand jury issues the indictment, the accused (i.e., defendant) is summoned to court or arrested (if not already in custody). The next step is an arraignment, a proceeding in which the defendant is brought before a judge, told of the charges they are accused of, and asked to plead guilty or not guilty. If the defendant's plea is guilty, a time is set for the defendant to return to court to be sentenced.

If the defendant pleads "not guilty," the time is set for the trial.

A defendant may enter a plea bargain with the prosecution--usually by agreeing to plead guilty to some but not all charges or lesser charges. The prosecution drops the remaining charges.

About nine out of ten defendants in criminal cases plead guilty.

Investigation

In a criminal case, a defense lawyer conducts a thorough investigation before trial, interviewing witnesses, visiting the crime scene, and examining physical evidence. An important part of this investigation is determining whether the evidence the government plans to use to prove its case was obtained legally.

The Fourth Amendment to the Constitution forbids unreasonable searches and seizures. To enforce this protection, the Supreme Court has decided that illegally seized evidence cannot be used at trial for most purposes.

For example, if the police seize evidence from a defendant's home without a search warrant, the lawyer for the defendant can ask the court to exclude the evidence from use at trial. The court holds a hearing to determine whether the search was unreasonable.

If the court rules that key evidence was seized illegally and cannot be used, the government often drops the charges against the defendant.

If the government has a strong case and the court ruled that the evidence was obtained legally, the defendant may decide to plead guilty rather than go to trial, where a conviction is likely.

Deliberations and verdict

After receiving its instructions from the judge, the jury retires to the jury room to discuss the evidence and reach a verdict (a decision on the factual issues). A criminal jury verdict must be unanimous; all jurors must agree that the defendant is guilty or not guilty.

If the jurors cannot agree, the judge declares a mistrial, and the prosecutor must decide whether to ask the court to dismiss the case or have it presented to another jury.

Judgment and sentencing

In federal criminal cases, if the jury (or judge, if there is no jury) decides that the defendant is guilty, the judge sets a date for a sentencing hearing. In federal criminal cases, the jury does not decide whether the defendant will go to prison or for how long; the judge does.

In federal death penalty cases, the jury does decide whether the defendant will receive a death sentence. Sentencing statutes passed by Congress control the judge's sentencing decision. Additionally, judges use Sentencing Guidelines, issued by the U.S. Sentencing Commission, as a source of advice as to the proper sentence. The guidelines consider the nature of the offense and the offender's criminal history.

A presentence report, prepared by one of the court's probation officers, provides the judge with information about the offender and the offense, including the sentence recommended by the guidelines. After determining the sentence, the judge signs a judgment, including the plea, the verdict, and sentence.

Right to appeal

A defendant who is found guilty in a federal criminal trial has a right to appeal the decision to the U.S. court of appeals, that is, ask the court of appeals to review the case to determine whether the trial was conducted properly. The grounds for appeal are usually that the district judge is said to have made an error, either in a procedure (admitting improper evidence, for example) or interpreting the law.

A defendant who pled guilty may not appeal the conviction.

A defendant who pled guilty may have the right to appeal their sentence.

The government may not appeal if a defendant in a criminal case is found not guilty because the Double Jeopardy Clause of the Fifth Amendment to the Constitution provides that no person shall "be twice put in jeopardy of life or limb" for the same offense.

This reflects society's belief that, even if a subsequent trial might finally find a defendant guilty, it is not proper for the government to harass an acquitted defendant through repeated retrials.

However, the government may sometimes appeal a sentence.

Notes for active learning

How Civil and Criminal Appeals Move Through the Federal Courts

- Assignment of Judges
- Alternative Dispute Resolution (ADR)
- Review of Lower Court Decision
- Oral Argument
- Decision
- The Supreme Court of the United States

Assignment of judges

The courts of appeals usually assign cases to a panel of three judges. The panel decides the case for the entire court. Sometimes, when the parties request it or a question of unusual importance, the judges on the appeals court assemble *en banc* (a rare event).

Review of a lower court decision

In making its decision, the panel reviews key parts of the record. The record consists of the documents filed in the case at trial and the transcript of the trial proceedings. The panel learns about the lawyers' legal arguments from the lawyers' briefs.

Briefs are written documents that each side submits to explain its case and tell why the court should decide in its favor.

Oral argument

If the court permits oral argument, the lawyers for each side have a limited amount of time (typically between 15 to 30 minutes) to argue (i.e., advocate and explain) their case to the judges (or justices at the highest court in the jurisdiction) in a formal courtroom session. The judges (or justices for the highest court in the jurisdiction) frequently question the attorneys about the relevant law as it applies to the facts and issues in the case before them.

A court of appeals differs from the federal trial courts. There are no jurors, witnesses, or court reporters. The lawyers for each side, but not the parties, are usually present in the courtroom.

Decision

After the submission of briefs and oral arguments, the judges discuss the case privately, consider relevant *precedents* (court decisions from higher courts in prior cases with similar facts and legal issues), and reach a decision. Courts are required to follow precedents.

For example, a U.S. court of appeals must follow the U.S. Supreme Court's decisions; a district court must follow the decisions of the U.S. Supreme Court and the decisions of the court of appeals of its circuit.

Courts are influenced by decisions they are not required to follow, such as the decisions of other circuits. Courts follow precedent unless they set forth reasons for the diversion.

At least two of the three judges on the panel must agree on a decision. One judge who agrees with the decision is chosen to write an opinion, which announces and explains the decision.

If a judge on the panel disagrees with the majority's opinion, the judge may write a dissent, giving reasons for disagreeing.

Many appellate opinions are published in books of opinions, called reporters. The opinions are read carefully by other judges and lawyers looking for precedents to guide them in their cases.

The accumulated judicial opinions make up a body of law known as *case law*, which is usually an accurate predictor of how future cases will be decided.

For decisions that the judges believe are important to the parties and contribute little to the law, the appeals courts frequently use short, unsigned opinions that often are not published.

If the court of appeals decides that the trial judge incorrectly interpreted the law or followed incorrect procedures, it reverses the district court's decision.

For example, the court of appeals could hold that the district judge allowed the jury to base its decision on evidence that never should have been admitted, and thus the defendant cannot be guilty.

Most of the time, courts of appeals uphold, rather than the reverse, district court decisions.

Sometimes when a higher court reverses the decision of the district court, it sends the case back (i.e., *remand* the case) to the lower court for another trial.

For example, *Miranda v. Arizona* case (1966), the Supreme Court ruled 5-4 that Ernesto Miranda's confession could not be used as evidence because he had not been advised of his right to remain silent or of his right to have a lawyer present during questioning.

However, the government did have other evidence against him. The case was remanded for a new trial, in which the improperly obtained confession was not used as evidence, but the other evidence convicted Miranda.

The Supreme Court of the United States

The Supreme Court is the highest in the nation. It is a different kind of appeals court; its major function is not correcting errors made by trial judges but clarifying the law in cases of national importance or when lower courts disagree about interpreting the Constitution or federal laws.

The Supreme Court does not have to hear every case that it is asked to review. Each year, losing parties ask the Supreme Court to review about 8,000 cases.

Almost all cases come to the Court as a *petition for writ of certiorari*. The court selects only about 80 to 120 of the most significant cases to review with oral arguments.

Supreme Court decisions establish a precedent for interpreting the Constitution and federal laws; holdings that state and federal courts must follow.

The power of judicial review makes the Supreme Court's role in our government vital. Judicial review is the power of a court when deciding a case to declare that a law passed by a legislature or action by the executive branch is invalid because it is inconsistent with the Constitution.

Although district courts, courts of appeals, and state courts can exercise the power of judicial review, their decisions about federal law are always subject, on appeal, to review by the Supreme Court.

When the Supreme Court declares a law unconstitutional, its decision can only be overruled by a later decision of the Supreme Court or Amendment to the Constitution.

Seven of the twenty-seven Amendments to the Constitution have invalidated the decisions of the Supreme Court. However, most Supreme Court cases do not concern the constitutionality of laws, but the interpretation of laws passed by Congress.

Although Congress has steadily increased the number of district and appeals court judges over the years, the Supreme Court has remained the same size since 1869. It consists of a Chief Justice and eight associate justices.

Like the federal court of appeals and federal district judges, the Supreme Court justices are appointed by the President with the Senate's *advice and consent*.

Unlike the judges in the courts of appeals, Supreme Court justices never sit on panels. Absent recusal, nine justices hear cases, and a majority ruling decides cases.

The Supreme Court begins its annual session, or term, on the first Monday of October. The term lasts until the Court has announced its decisions in cases where it has heard an argument that term—usually late June or early July.

During the term, the Court, sitting for two weeks at a time, hears oral arguments on Monday through Wednesday and holds private conferences to discuss the cases, reach decisions, and begin preparing the written opinions that explain its decisions.

Most decisions and opinions are released in the late spring and early summer.

Standards of review for federal courts

Standard of review	De novo	Clearly erroneous	Abuse of discretion
Type of decision under review	Question of the law	Question of fact	Discretionary action
Lower-court decision maker	Trial judge	Trial judge	Trial judge
Deference given to lower court	No deference	Substantial deference	Extreme deference
Party typically benefitted	Appellant	Appellee	Appellee
Definition	An appellate court reviews the legal question anew and independently, without regard to the conclusions reached by the trial court. "When *de novo* review is compelled, no form of appellate deference is acceptable." *Salve Regina College v. Russell*, (1991).	A finding is 'clearly erroneous' when although there is evidence to support it, the reviewing court on the entire evidence is left with the definite and firm conviction that a mistake has been committed. *United States v. United States Gypsum Co.*, (1948) "If the district court's account of the evidence is plausible in light of the record viewed in its entirety, the court of appeals may not reverse it even though convinced that had it been sitting as the trier of fact, it would have weighed the evidence differently. When there are two permissible views of the evidence, the factfinder's choice between them cannot be clearly erroneous." *Anderson v. Bessemer City*, (1985).	Generally, an abuse of discretion only occurs where no reasonable person could take the view adopted by the trial court. If reasonable persons could differ, no abuse of discretion can be found. *Harrington v. DeVito*, (7th Cir. 1981) Under the abuse of discretion standard, a trial court's decision will not be disturbed unless the appellate court has a definite and firm conviction that the lower court made a clear error of judgment or exceeded the bounds of permissible choice in the circumstances. We will not alter a trial court's decision unless it can be shown that the court's decision was an arbitrary, capricious, whimsical, or manifestly unreasonable judgment. *Wright v. Abbott Laboratories, Inc.*. (10th Cir. 2001)
Examples	Motions for summary judgment, constitutional questions, statutory interpretation	Questions regarding who did what, where, and when; questions of intent and motive; questions of ultimate fact (such as negligence)	Rule 11 sanctions, attorney's fees, courtroom management, motions to compel, injunctions, and temporary restraining orders.

The Constitution of the United States (*a transcription*)

THE U.S. NATIONAL ARCHIVES & RECORDS ADMINISTRATION
www.archives.gov

The following text is a transcription of the Constitution as it was inscribed by Jacob Shallus on parchment (the document on display in the Rotunda at the National Archives Museum.) The spelling and punctuation reflect the original.

The Constitution of the United States: A Transcription

The following text is a transcription of the Constitution as it was inscribed by Jacob Shallus on parchment (displayed in the Rotunda at the National Archives Museum.) The authenticated text of the Constitution can be found on the website of the Government Printing Office.

We the People of the United States, in Order to form a more perfect Union, establish Justice, insure domestic Tranquility, provide for the common defence, promote the general Welfare, and secure the Blessings of Liberty to ourselves and our Posterity, do ordain and establish this Constitution for the United States of America.

Article. I

Section. 1.

All legislative Powers herein granted shall be vested in a Congress of the United States, which shall consist of a Senate and House of Representatives.

Section. 2.

The House of Representatives shall be composed of Members chosen every second Year by the People of the several States, and the Electors in each State shall have the Qualifications requisite for Electors of the most numerous Branch of the State Legislature.

No Person shall be a Representative who shall not have attained to the Age of twenty five Years, and been seven Years a Citizen of the United States, and who shall not, when elected, be an Inhabitant of that State in which he shall be chosen.

Representatives and direct Taxes shall be apportioned among the several States which may be included within this Union, according to their respective Numbers, which shall be determined by adding to the whole Number of free Persons, including those bound to Service for a Term of Years, and excluding Indians not taxed, three fifths of all other Persons. The actual Enumeration shall be made within three Years after the first Meeting of the Congress of the United States, and within every subsequent Term of ten Years, in such Manner as they shall by Law direct. The Number of Representatives shall not exceed one for every thirty Thousand, but each State shall have at Least one Representative; and until such enumeration shall be made, the State of New Hampshire shall be entitled to chuse three, Massachusetts eight, Rhode-Island and Providence

Plantations one, Connecticut five, New-York six, New Jersey four, Pennsylvania eight, Delaware one, Maryland six, Virginia ten, North Carolina five, South Carolina five, and Georgia three.

When vacancies happen in the Representation from any State, the Executive Authority thereof shall issue Writs of Election to fill such Vacancies.

The House of Representatives shall chuse their Speaker and other Officers; and shall have the sole Power of Impeachment.

Section. 3.

The Senate of the United States shall be composed of two Senators from each State, chosen by the Legislature thereof, for six Years; and each Senator shall have one Vote.

Immediately after they shall be assembled in Consequence of the first Election, they shall be divided as equally as may be into three Classes. The Seats of the Senators of the first Class shall be vacated at the Expiration of the second Year, of the second Class at the Expiration of the fourth Year, and of the third Class at the Expiration of the sixth Year, so that one third may be chosen every second Year; and if Vacancies happen by Resignation, or otherwise, during the Recess of the Legislature of any State, the Executive thereof may make temporary Appointments until the next Meeting of the Legislature, which shall then fill such Vacancies.

No Person shall be a Senator who shall not have attained to the Age of thirty Years, and been nine Years a Citizen of the United States, and who shall not, when elected, be an Inhabitant of that State for which he shall be chosen.

The Vice President of the United States shall be President of the Senate, but shall have no Vote, unless they be equally divided.

The Senate shall chuse their other Officers, and also a President pro tempore, in the Absence of the Vice President, or when he shall exercise the Office of President of the United States.

The Senate shall have the sole Power to try all Impeachments. When sitting for that Purpose, they shall be on Oath or Affirmation. When the President of the United States is tried, the Chief Justice shall preside: And no Person shall be convicted without the Concurrence of two thirds of the Members present.

Judgment in Cases of Impeachment shall not extend further than to removal from Office, and disqualification to hold and enjoy any Office of honor, Trust or Profit under the United States: but the Party convicted shall nevertheless be liable and subject to Indictment, Trial, Judgment and Punishment, according to Law.

Section. 4.

The Times, Places and Manner of holding Elections for Senators and Representatives, shall be prescribed in each State by the Legislature thereof; but the Congress may at any time by Law make or alter such Regulations, except as to the Places of chusing Senators.

The Congress shall assemble at least once in every Year, and such Meeting shall be on the first Monday in December, unless they shall by Law appoint a different Day.

Section. 5.

Each House shall be the Judge of the Elections, Returns and Qualifications of its own Members, and a Majority of each shall constitute a Quorum to do Business; but a smaller Number may adjourn from day to day, and may be authorized to compel the Attendance of absent Members, in such Manner, and under such Penalties as each House may provide.

Each House may determine the Rules of its Proceedings, punish its Members for disorderly Behaviour, and, with the Concurrence of two thirds, expel a Member.

Each House shall keep a Journal of its Proceedings, and from time to time publish the same, excepting such Parts as may in their Judgment require Secrecy; and the Yeas and Nays of the Members of either House on any question shall, at the Desire of one fifth of those Present, be entered on the Journal.

Neither House, during the Session of Congress, shall, without the Consent of the other, adjourn for more than three days, nor to any other Place than that in which the two Houses shall be sitting.

Section. 6.

The Senators and Representatives shall receive a Compensation for their Services, to be ascertained by Law, and paid out of the Treasury of the United States. They shall in all Cases, except Treason, Felony and Breach of the Peace, be privileged from Arrest during their Attendance at the Session of their respective Houses, and in going to and returning from the same; and for any Speech or Debate in either House, they shall not be questioned in any other Place.

No Senator or Representative shall, during the Time for which he was elected, be appointed to any civil Office under the Authority of the United States, which shall have been created, or the Emoluments whereof shall have been encreased during such time; and no Person holding any Office under the United States, shall be a Member of either House during his Continuance in Office.

Section. 7.

All Bills for raising Revenue shall originate in the House of Representatives; but the Senate may propose or concur with Amendments as on other Bills.

Every Bill which shall have passed the House of Representatives and the Senate, shall, before it become a Law, be presented to the President of the United States; If he approves he shall sign it, but if not he shall return it, with his Objections to that House in which it shall have originated, who shall enter the Objections at large on their Journal, and proceed to reconsider it. If after such Reconsideration two thirds of that House shall agree to pass the Bill, it shall be sent, together with the Objections, to the other House, by which it shall likewise be reconsidered, and if approved by two thirds of that House, it shall become a Law. But in all such Cases the Votes of both Houses shall be determined by yeas and Nays, and the Names of the Persons voting for and against the Bill shall be entered on the Journal of each House respectively. If any Bill shall not be returned by the President within ten Days (Sundays excepted) after it shall have been presented to him, the Same shall be a Law, in like Manner as if he had signed it, unless the Congress by their Adjournment prevent its Return, in which Case it shall not be a Law.

Every Order, Resolution, or Vote to which the Concurrence of the Senate and House of Representatives may be necessary (except on a question of Adjournment) shall be presented to the President of the United States; and before the Same shall take Effect, shall be approved by him, or being disapproved by him, shall be repassed by two thirds of the Senate and House of Representatives, according to the Rules and Limitations prescribed in the Case of a Bill.

Section. 8.

The Congress shall have Power To lay and collect Taxes, Duties, Imposts and Excises, to pay the Debts and provide for the common Defence and general Welfare of the United States; but all Duties, Imposts and Excises shall be uniform throughout the United States;

To borrow Money on the credit of the United States;

To regulate Commerce with foreign Nations, and among the several States, and with the Indian Tribes;

To establish an uniform Rule of Naturalization, and uniform Laws on the subject of Bankruptcies throughout the United States;

To coin Money, regulate the Value thereof, and of foreign Coin, and fix the Standard of Weights and Measures;

To provide for the Punishment of counterfeiting the Securities and current Coin of the United States;

To establish Post Offices and post Roads;

To promote the Progress of Science and useful Arts, by securing for limited Times to Authors and Inventors the exclusive Right to their respective Writings and Discoveries;

To constitute Tribunals inferior to the Supreme Court;

To define and punish Piracies and Felonies committed on the high Seas, and Offences against the Law of Nations;

To declare War, grant Letters of Marque and Reprisal, and make Rules concerning Captures on Land and Water;

To raise and support Armies, but no Appropriation of Money to that Use shall be for a longer Term than two Years;

To provide and maintain a Navy;

To make Rules for the Government and Regulation of the land and naval Forces;

To provide for calling forth the Militia to execute the Laws of the Union, suppress Insurrections and repel Invasions;

To provide for organizing, arming, and disciplining, the Militia, and for governing such Part of them as may be employed in the Service of the United States, reserving to the States respectively, the Appointment of the Officers, and the Authority of training the Militia according to the discipline prescribed by Congress;

To exercise exclusive Legislation in all Cases whatsoever, over such District (not exceeding ten Miles square) as may, by Cession of particular States, and the Acceptance of Congress, become the Seat of the Government of the United States, and to exercise like Authority over all Places purchased by the Consent of the Legislature of the State in which the Same shall be, for the Erection of Forts, Magazines, Arsenals, dock-Yards, and other needful Buildings;—And

To make all Laws which shall be necessary and proper for carrying into Execution the foregoing Powers, and all other Powers vested by this Constitution in the Government of the United States, or in any Department or Officer thereof.

Section. 9.

The Migration or Importation of such Persons as any of the States now existing shall think proper to admit, shall not be prohibited by the Congress prior to the Year one thousand eight hundred and eight, but a Tax or duty may be imposed on such Importation, not exceeding ten dollars for each Person.

The Privilege of the Writ of Habeas Corpus shall not be suspended, unless when in Cases of Rebellion or Invasion the public Safety may require it.

No Bill of Attainder or ex post facto Law shall be passed.

No Capitation, or other direct, Tax shall be laid, unless in Proportion to the Census or enumeration herein before directed to be taken.

No Tax or Duty shall be laid on Articles exported from any State.

No Preference shall be given by any Regulation of Commerce or Revenue to the Ports of one State over those of another: nor shall Vessels bound to, or from, one State, be obliged to enter, clear, or pay Duties in another.

No Money shall be drawn from the Treasury, but in Consequence of Appropriations made by Law; and a regular Statement and Account of the Receipts and Expenditures of all public Money shall be published from time to time.

No Title of Nobility shall be granted by the United States: And no Person holding any Office of Profit or Trust under them, shall, without the Consent of the Congress, accept of any present, Emolument, Office, or Title, of any kind whatever, from any King, Prince, or foreign State.

Section. 10.

No State shall enter into any Treaty, Alliance, or Confederation; grant Letters of Marque and Reprisal; coin Money; emit Bills of Credit; make any Thing but gold and silver Coin a Tender in Payment of Debts; pass any Bill of Attainder, ex post facto Law, or Law impairing the Obligation of Contracts, or grant any Title of Nobility.

No State shall, without the Consent of the Congress, lay any Imposts or Duties on Imports or Exports, except what may be absolutely necessary for executing it's inspection Laws: and the net

Produce of all Duties and Imposts, laid by any State on Imports or Exports, shall be for the Use of the Treasury of the United States; and all such Laws shall be subject to the Revision and Controul of the Congress.

No State shall, without the Consent of Congress, lay any Duty of Tonnage, keep Troops, or Ships of War in time of Peace, enter into any Agreement or Compact with another State, or with a foreign Power, or engage in War, unless actually invaded, or in such imminent Danger as will not admit of delay.

Article. II

Section. 1.

The executive Power shall be vested in a President of the United States of America. He shall hold his Office during the Term of four Years, and, together with the Vice President, chosen for the same Term, be elected, as follows

Each State shall appoint, in such Manner as the Legislature thereof may direct, a Number of Electors, equal to the whole Number of Senators and Representatives to which the State may be entitled in the Congress: but no Senator or Representative, or Person holding an Office of Trust or Profit under the United States, shall be appointed an Elector.

The Electors shall meet in their respective States, and vote by Ballot for two Persons, of whom one at least shall not be an Inhabitant of the same State with themselves. And they shall make a List of all the Persons voted for, and of the Number of Votes for each; which List they shall sign and certify, and transmit sealed to the Seat of the Government of the United States, directed to the President of the Senate. The President of the Senate shall, in the Presence of the Senate and House of Representatives, open all the Certificates, and the Votes shall then be counted. The Person having the greatest Number of Votes shall be the President, if such Number be a Majority of the whole Number of Electors appointed; and if there be more than one who have such Majority, and have an equal Number of Votes, then the House of Representatives shall immediately chuse by Ballot one of them for President; and if no Person have a Majority, then from the five highest on the List the said House shall in like Manner chuse the President. But in chusing the President, the Votes shall be taken by States, the Representation from each State having one Vote; A quorum for this Purpose shall consist of a Member or Members from two thirds of the States, and a Majority of all the States shall be necessary to a Choice. In every Case, after the Choice of the President, the Person having the greatest Number of Votes of the Electors shall be the Vice President. But if there should remain two or more who have equal Votes, the Senate shall chuse from them by Ballot the Vice President.

The Congress may determine the Time of chusing the Electors, and the Day on which they shall give their Votes; which Day shall be the same throughout the United States.

No Person except a natural born Citizen, or a Citizen of the United States, at the time of the Adoption of this Constitution, shall be eligible to the Office of President; neither shall any Person be eligible to that Office who shall not have attained to the Age of thirty five Years, and been fourteen Years a Resident within the United States.

In Case of the Removal of the President from Office, or of his Death, Resignation, or Inability to discharge the Powers and Duties of the said Office, the Same shall devolve on the Vice President, and the Congress may by Law provide for the Case of Removal, Death, Resignation or Inability, both of the President and Vice President, declaring what Officer shall then act as President, and such Officer shall act accordingly, until the Disability be removed, or a President shall be elected.

The President shall, at stated Times, receive for his Services, a Compensation, which shall neither be encreased nor diminished during the Period for which he shall have been elected, and he shall not receive within that Period any other Emolument from the United States, or any of them.

Before he enters on the Execution of his Office, he shall take the following Oath or Affirmation:—"I do solemnly swear (or affirm) that I will faithfully execute the Office of President of the United States, and will to the best of my Ability, preserve, protect and defend the Constitution of the United States."

Section. 2.

The President shall be Commander in Chief of the Army and Navy of the United States, and of the Militia of the several States, when called into the actual Service of the United States; he may require the Opinion, in writing, of the principal Officer in each of the executive Departments, upon any Subject relating to the Duties of their respective Offices, and he shall have Power to grant Reprieves and Pardons for Offences against the United States, except in Cases of Impeachment.

He shall have Power, by and with the Advice and Consent of the Senate, to make Treaties, provided two thirds of the Senators present concur; and he shall nominate, and by and with the Advice and Consent of the Senate, shall appoint Ambassadors, other public Ministers and Consuls, Judges of the supreme Court, and all other Officers of the United States, whose Appointments are not herein otherwise provided for, and which shall be established by Law: but the Congress may by Law vest the Appointment of such inferior Officers, as they think proper, in the President alone, in the Courts of Law, or in the Heads of Departments.

The President shall have Power to fill up all Vacancies that may happen during the Recess of the Senate, by granting Commissions which shall expire at the End of their next Session.

Section. 3.

He shall from time to time give to the Congress Information of the State of the Union, and recommend to their Consideration such Measures as he shall judge necessary and expedient; he may, on extraordinary Occasions, convene both Houses, or either of them, and in Case of Disagreement between them, with Respect to the Time of Adjournment, he may adjourn them to such Time as he shall think proper; he shall receive Ambassadors and other public Ministers; he shall take Care that the Laws be faithfully executed, and shall Commission all the Officers of the United States.

Section. 4.

The President, Vice President and all civil Officers of the United States, shall be removed from Office on Impeachment for, and Conviction of, Treason, Bribery, or other high Crimes and Misdemeanors.

Article III

Section. 1.

The judicial Power of the United States, shall be vested in one supreme Court, and in such inferior Courts as the Congress may from time to time ordain and establish. The Judges, both of the supreme and inferior Courts, shall hold their Offices during good Behaviour, and shall, at stated Times, receive for their Services, a Compensation, which shall not be diminished during their Continuance in Office.

Section. 2.

The judicial Power shall extend to all Cases, in Law and Equity, arising under this Constitution, the Laws of the United States, and Treaties made, or which shall be made, under their Authority;—to all Cases affecting Ambassadors, other public Ministers and Consuls;—to all Cases of admiralty and maritime Jurisdiction;—to Controversies to which the United States shall be a Party;—to Controversies between two or more States;—between a State and Citizens of another State,—between Citizens of different States,—between Citizens of the same State claiming Lands under Grants of different States, and between a State, or the Citizens thereof, and foreign States, Citizens or Subjects.

In all Cases affecting Ambassadors, other public Ministers and Consuls, and those in which a State shall be Party, the supreme Court shall have original Jurisdiction. In all the other Cases before mentioned, the supreme Court shall have appellate Jurisdiction, both as to Law and Fact, with such Exceptions, and under such Regulations as the Congress shall make.

The Trial of all Crimes, except in Cases of Impeachment, shall be by Jury; and such Trial shall be held in the State where the said Crimes shall have been committed; but when not committed within any State, the Trial shall be at such Place or Places as the Congress may by Law have directed.

Section. 3.

Treason against the United States, shall consist only in levying War against them, or in adhering to their Enemies, giving them Aid and Comfort. No Person shall be convicted of Treason unless on the Testimony of two Witnesses to the same overt Act, or on Confession in open Court.

The Congress shall have Power to declare the Punishment of Treason, but no Attainder of Treason shall work Corruption of Blood, or Forfeiture except during the Life of the Person attainted.

Article. IV

Section. 1.

Full Faith and Credit shall be given in each State to the public Acts, Records, and judicial Proceedings of every other State. And the Congress may by general Laws prescribe the Manner in which such Acts, Records and Proceedings shall be proved, and the Effect thereof.

Section. 2.

The Citizens of each State shall be entitled to all Privileges and Immunities of Citizens in the several States.

A Person charged in any State with Treason, Felony, or other Crime, who shall flee from Justice, and be found in another State, shall on Demand of the executive Authority of the State from which he fled, be delivered up, to be removed to the State having Jurisdiction of the Crime.

No Person held to Service or Labour in one State, under the Laws thereof, escaping into another, shall, in Consequence of any Law or Regulation therein, be discharged from such Service or Labour, but shall be delivered up on Claim of the Party to whom such Service or Labour may be due.

Section. 3.

New States may be admitted by the Congress into this Union; but no new State shall be formed or erected within the Jurisdiction of any other State; nor any State be formed by the Junction of two or more States, or Parts of States, without the Consent of the Legislatures of the States concerned as well as of the Congress.

The Congress shall have Power to dispose of and make all needful Rules and Regulations respecting the Territory or other Property belonging to the United States; and nothing in this Constitution shall be so construed as to Prejudice any Claims of the United States, or of any particular State.

Section. 4.

The United States shall guarantee to every State in this Union a Republican Form of Government, and shall protect each of them against Invasion; and on Application of the Legislature, or of the Executive (when the Legislature cannot be convened), against domestic Violence.

Article. V

The Congress, whenever two thirds of both Houses shall deem it necessary, shall propose Amendments to this Constitution, or, on the Application of the Legislatures of two thirds of the several States, shall call a Convention for proposing Amendments, which, in either Case, shall be valid to all Intents and Purposes, as Part of this Constitution, when ratified by the Legislatures of three fourths of the several States, or by Conventions in three fourths thereof, as the one or the other Mode of Ratification may be proposed by the Congress; Provided that no Amendment which may be made prior to the Year One thousand eight hundred and eight shall in any Manner affect the first and fourth Clauses in the Ninth Section of the first Article; and that no State, without its Consent, shall be deprived of its equal Suffrage in the Senate.

Article. VI

All Debts contracted and Engagements entered into, before the Adoption of this Constitution, shall be as valid against the United States under this Constitution, as under the Confederation.

This Constitution, and the Laws of the United States which shall be made in Pursuance thereof; and all Treaties made, or which shall be made, under the Authority of the United States, shall be the supreme Law of the Land; and the Judges in every State shall be bound thereby, any Thing in the Constitution or Laws of any State to the Contrary notwithstanding.

The Senators and Representatives before mentioned, and the Members of the several State Legislatures, and all executive and judicial Officers, both of the United States and of the several States, shall be bound by Oath or Affirmation, to support this Constitution; but no religious Test shall ever be required as a Qualification to any Office or public Trust under the United States.

Article. VII

The Ratification of the Conventions of nine States, shall be sufficient for the Establishment of this Constitution between the States so ratifying the Same.

The Word, "the," being interlined between the seventh and eighth Lines of the first Page, The Word "Thirty" being partly written on an Erazure in the fifteenth Line of the first Page, The Words "is tried" being interlined between the thirty second and thirty third Lines of the first Page and the Word "the" being interlined between the forty third and forty fourth Lines of the second Page.

Attest William Jackson Secretary, done in Convention by the Unanimous Consent of the States present the Seventeenth Day of September in the Year of our Lord one thousand seven hundred and Eighty seven and of the Independance of the United States of America the Twelfth In witness whereof We have hereunto subscribed our Names, G°. Washington, *Presidt and deputy from Virginia*

Delaware
Geo: Read
Gunning Bedford jun
John Dickinson
Richard Bassett
Jaco: Broom

Maryland
James McHenry
Dan of St Thos. Jenifer
Danl. Carroll

Virginia
John Blair
James Madison Jr.

North Carolina
Wm. Blount
Richd. Dobbs Spaight
Hu Williamson

South Carolina
J. Rutledge
Charles Cotesworth Pinckney
Charles Pinckney
Pierce Butler

Georgia
William Few
Abr Baldwin

New Hampshire
John Langdon
Nicholas Gilman

Massachusetts
Nathaniel Gorham
Rufus King

Connecticut
Wm. Saml. Johnson
Roger Sherman

New York
Alexander Hamilton

New Jersey
Wil: Livingston
David Brearley
Wm. Paterson
Jona: Dayton

Pensylvania
B Franklin
Thomas Mifflin
Robt. Morris
Geo. Clymer
Thos. FitzSimons
Jared Ingersoll
James Wilson
Gouv Morris

Enactment of the Bill of Rights of the United States of America (1791)

The first ten Amendments to the Constitution make up the Bill of Rights. Written by James Madison in response to calls from several states for greater constitutional protection for individual liberties, the Bill of Rights lists specific prohibitions on governmental power. The Virginia Declaration of Rights, written by George Mason, strongly influenced Madison.

One of the contention points between Federalists and Anti-Federalists was the Constitution's lack of a bill of rights that would place specific limits on government power.

Federalists argued that the Constitution did not need a bill of rights because the people and the states kept powers not explicitly given to the federal government.

Anti-Federalists held that a *bill of rights* was necessary to safeguard individual liberty.

Madison, then a member of the U.S. House of Representatives, went through the Constitution itself, making changes where he thought most appropriate.

Several Representatives, led by Roger Sherman, objected that Congress had no authority to change the wording of the Constitution. Therefore, Madison's changes were presented as a list of amendments that would follow Article VII.

The House approved 17 amendments. Of these 17, the Senate approved 12. Those 12 were sent to the states for approval in August of 1789. Of those 12 proposed amendments, 10 were quickly ratified. Virginia's legislature became the last to ratify the Amendments on December 15, 1791. These Amendments are the Bill of Rights.

The Bill of Rights is a list of limits on government power. For example, what the Founders saw as the natural right of individuals to speak and worship freely was protected by the First Amendment's prohibitions on Congress from making laws establishing a religion or abridging freedom of speech.

Another example is the natural right to be free from the government's unreasonable intrusion in one's home was safeguarded by the Fourth Amendment's warrant requirements.

Other precursors to the Bill of Rights include English documents such as the Magna Carta[1], the Petition of Rights, the English Bill of Rights, and the Massachusetts Body of Liberties.

The Magna Carta illustrates Compact Theory[1] as well as initial strides toward limited government. Its provisions address individual rights and political rights. Latin for "Great Charter," the Magna Carta was written by Barons in Runnymede, England, and forced on the King.

Although the protections were generally limited to the prerogatives of the Barons, the Magna Carta embodied the general principle that the King accepted limitations on his rule. These included the fundamental acknowledgment that the king was not above the law.

Included in the Magna Carta are protections for the English church, petitioning the king, freedom from the forced quarter of troops and unreasonable searches, due process and fair trial protections, and freedom from excessive fines. These protections can be found in the First, Third, Fourth, Fifth, Sixth, and Eighth Amendments to the Constitution.

The Magna Carta is the oldest compact in England. The Mayflower Compact, the Fundamental Orders of Connecticut, and the Albany Plan are examples from the American colonies.

The Articles of Confederation was a compact among the states, and the Constitution creates a compact based on a federal system between the national government, state governments, and the people. The Hayne-Webster Debate focused on the compact created by the Constitution.

---

[1] Philosophers including Thomas Hobbes, John Locke, and Jean-Jacques Rousseau theorized that peoples' condition in a "state of nature" (that is, outside of society) is one of freedom, but that freedom inevitably degrades into war, chaos, or debilitating competition without the benefit of a system of laws and government. They reasoned, therefore, that for their happiness, individuals willingly trade some of their natural freedom in exchange for the protections provided by the government.

The Bill of Rights: Amendments I–X

Amendment I

Congress shall make no law respecting an establishment of religion, or prohibiting the free exercise thereof; or abridging the freedom of speech, or of the press; or the right of the people peaceably to assemble, and to petition the government for a redress of grievances.

Amendment II

A well regulated militia, being necessary to the security of a free state, the right of the people to keep and bear arms, shall not be infringed.

Amendment III

No soldier shall, in time of peace be quartered in any house, without the consent of the owner, nor in time of war, but in a manner to be prescribed by law.

Amendment IV

The right of the people to be secure in their persons, houses, papers, and effects, against unreasonable searches and seizures, shall not be violated, and no warrants shall issue, but upon probable cause, supported by oath or affirmation, and particularly describing the place to be searched, and the persons or things to be seized.

Amendment V

No person shall be held to answer for a capital, or otherwise infamous crime, unless on a presentment or indictment of a grand jury, except in cases arising in the land or naval forces, or in the militia, when in actual service in time of war or public danger; nor shall any person be subject for the same offense to be twice put in jeopardy of life or limb; nor shall be compelled in any criminal case to be a witness against himself, nor be deprived of life, liberty, or property, without due process of law; nor shall private property be taken for public use, without just compensation.

Amendment VI

In all criminal prosecutions, the accused shall enjoy the right to a speedy and public trial, by an impartial jury of the state and district wherein the crime shall have been committed, which district shall have been previously ascertained by law, and to be informed of the nature and cause of the accusation; to be confronted with the witnesses against him; to have compulsory process for obtaining witnesses in his favor, and to have the assistance of counsel for his defense.

Amendment VII

In suits at common law, where the value in controversy shall exceed twenty dollars, the right of trial by jury shall be preserved, and no fact tried by a jury, shall be otherwise reexamined in any court of the United States, than according to the rules of the common law.

Amendment VIII

Excessive bail shall not be required, nor excessive fines imposed, nor cruel and unusual punishments inflicted.

Amendment IX

The enumeration in the Constitution, of certain rights, shall not be construed to deny or disparage others retained by the people.

Amendment X

The powers not delegated to the United States by the Constitution, nor prohibited by it to the states, are reserved to the states respectively, or to the people.

Constitutional Amendments XI–XXVII

AMENDMENT XI

Passed by Congress March 4, 1794. Ratified February 7, 1795.

Note: Article III, section 2, of the Constitution was modified by amendment 11.

The Judicial power of the United States shall not be construed to extend to any suit in law or equity, commenced or prosecuted against one of the United States by Citizens of another State, or by Citizens or Subjects of any Foreign State.

AMENDMENT XII

Passed by Congress December 9, 1803. Ratified June 15, 1804.

Note: A portion of Article II, section 1 of the Constitution was superseded by the 12th amendment.

The Electors shall meet in their respective states and vote by ballot for President and Vice-President, one of whom, at least, shall not be an inhabitant of the same state with themselves; they shall name in their ballots the person voted for as President, and in distinct ballots the person voted for as Vice-President, and they shall make distinct lists of all persons voted for as President, and of all persons voted for as Vice-President, and of the number of votes for each, which lists they shall sign and certify, and transmit sealed to the seat of the government of the United States, directed to the President of the Senate; -- the President of the Senate shall, in the presence of the Senate and House of Representatives, open all the certificates and the votes shall then be counted; -- The person having the greatest number of votes for President, shall be the President, if such number be a majority of the whole number of Electors appointed; and if no person have such majority, then from the persons having the highest numbers not exceeding three on the list of those voted for as President, the House of Representatives shall choose immediately, by ballot, the President. But in choosing the President, the votes shall be taken by states, the representation from each state having one vote; a quorum for this purpose shall consist of a member or members from two-thirds of the states, and a majority of all the states shall be necessary to a choice. [And if the House of Representatives shall not choose a President whenever the right of choice shall devolve upon them, before the fourth day of March next following, then the Vice-President shall act as President, as in case of the death or other constitutional disability of the President. --]* The person having the greatest number of votes as Vice-President, shall be the Vice-President, if such number be a majority of the whole number of Electors appointed, and if no person have a majority, then from the two highest numbers on the list, the Senate shall choose the Vice-President; a quorum for the purpose shall consist of two-thirds of the whole number of Senators, and a majority of the whole number shall be necessary to a choice. But no person constitutionally ineligible to the office of President shall be eligible to that of Vice-President of the United States.

*Superseded by section 3 of the 20th Amendment.

AMENDMENT XIII

Passed by Congress January 31, 1865. Ratified December 6, 1865.

Note: A portion of Article IV, section 2, of the Constitution was superseded by the 13th amendment.

Section 1.
Neither slavery nor involuntary servitude, except as a punishment for crime whereof the party shall have been duly convicted, shall exist within the United States, or any place subject to their jurisdiction.

Section 2.
Congress shall have power to enforce this article by appropriate legislation.

AMENDMENT XIV

Passed by Congress June 13, 1866. Ratified July 9, 1868.

Note: Article I, section 2, of the Constitution was modified by section 2 of the 14th amendment.

Section 1.
All persons born or naturalized in the United States, and subject to the jurisdiction thereof, are citizens of the United States and of the State wherein they reside. No State shall make or enforce any law which shall abridge the privileges or immunities of citizens of the United States; nor shall any State deprive any person of life, liberty, or property, without due process of law; nor deny to any person within its jurisdiction the equal protection of the laws.

Section 2.
Representatives shall be apportioned among the several States according to their respective numbers, counting the whole number of persons in each State, excluding Indians not taxed. But when the right to vote at any election for the choice of electors for President and Vice-President of the United States, Representatives in Congress, the Executive and Judicial officers of a State, or the members of the Legislature thereof, is denied to any of the male inhabitants of such State, being twenty-one years of age,* and citizens of the United States, or in any way abridged, except for participation in rebellion, or other crime, the basis of representation therein shall be reduced in the proportion which the number of such male citizens shall bear to the whole number of male citizens twenty-one years of age in such State.

Section 3.
No person shall be a Senator or Representative in Congress, or elector of President and Vice-President, or hold any office, civil or military, under the United States, or under any State, who, having previously taken an oath, as a member of Congress, or as an officer of the United States, or as a member of any State legislature, or as an executive or judicial officer of any State, to support the Constitution of the United States, shall have engaged in insurrection or rebellion against the same, or given aid or comfort to the enemies thereof. But Congress may by a vote of two-thirds of each House, remove such disability.

Section 4.

The validity of the public debt of the United States, authorized by law, including debts incurred for payment of pensions and bounties for services in suppressing insurrection or rebellion, shall not be questioned. But neither the United States nor any State shall assume or pay any debt or obligation incurred in aid of insurrection or rebellion against the United States, or any claim for the loss or emancipation of any slave; but all such debts, obligations and claims shall be held illegal and void.

Section 5.

The Congress shall have the power to enforce, by appropriate legislation, the provisions of this article.

Changed by section 1 of the 26th Amendment.

AMENDMENT XV

Passed by Congress February 26, 1869. Ratified February 3, 1870.

Section 1.

The right of citizens of the United States to vote shall not be denied or abridged by the United States or by any State on account of race, color, or previous condition of servitude.

Section 2.

The Congress shall have the power to enforce this article by appropriate legislation.

AMENDMENT XVI

Passed by Congress July 2, 1909. Ratified February 3, 1913.

Note: Article I, section 9, of the Constitution was modified by amendment 16.

The Congress shall have power to lay and collect taxes on incomes, from whatever source derived, without apportionment among the several States, and without regard to any census or enumeration.

AMENDMENT XVII

Passed by Congress May 13, 1912. Ratified April 8, 1913.

Note: Article I, section 3, of the Constitution was modified by the 17th Amendment.

The Senate of the United States shall be composed of two Senators from each State, elected by the people thereof, for six years; and each Senator shall have one vote. The electors in each State shall have the qualifications requisite for electors of the most numerous branch of the State legislatures.

When vacancies happen in the representation of any State in the Senate, the executive authority of such State shall issue writs of election to fill such vacancies: *Provided*, That the legislature of any State may empower the executive thereof to make temporary appointments until the people fill the vacancies by election as the legislature may direct.

This amendment shall not be so construed as to affect the election or term of any Senator chosen before it becomes valid as part of the Constitution.

AMENDMENT XVIII

Passed by Congress December 18, 1917. Ratified January 16, 1919. Repealed by Amendment 21.

Section 1.

After one year from the ratification of this article the manufacture, sale, or transportation of intoxicating liquors within, the importation thereof into, or the exportation thereof from the United States and all territory subject to the jurisdiction thereof for beverage purposes is hereby prohibited.

Section 2.

The Congress and the several States shall have concurrent power to enforce this article by appropriate legislation.

Section 3.

This article shall be inoperative unless it shall have been ratified as an amendment to the Constitution by the legislatures of the several States, as provided in the Constitution, within seven years from the date of the submission hereof to the States by the Congress.

AMENDMENT XIX

Passed by Congress June 4, 1919. Ratified August 18, 1920.

The right of citizens of the United States to vote shall not be denied or abridged by the United States or by any State on account of sex.

Congress shall have power to enforce this article by appropriate legislation.

AMENDMENT XX

Passed by Congress March 2, 1932. Ratified January 23, 1933.

Note: Article I, section 4, of the Constitution was modified by section 2 of this Amendment. In addition, a portion of the 12th Amendment was superseded by section 3.

Section 1.

The terms of the President and the Vice President shall end at noon on the 20th day of January, and the terms of Senators and Representatives at noon on the 3d day of January, of the years in which such terms would have ended if this article had not been ratified; and the terms of their successors shall then begin.

Section 2.

The Congress shall assemble at least once in every year, and such meeting shall begin at noon on the 3d day of January, unless they shall by law appoint a different day.

Section 3.

If, at the time fixed for the beginning of the term of the President, the President elect shall have died, the Vice President elect shall become President. If a President shall not have been chosen before the time fixed for the beginning of his term, or if the President elect shall have failed to qualify, then the Vice President elect shall act as President until a President shall have qualified; and the Congress may by law provide for the case wherein neither a President elect nor a Vice President elect shall have qualified, declaring who shall then act as President, or the manner in which one who is to act shall be selected, and such person shall act accordingly until a President or Vice President shall have qualified.

Section 4.

The Congress may by law provide for the case of the death of any of the persons from whom the House of Representatives may choose a President whenever the right of choice shall have devolved upon them, and for the case of the death of any of the persons from whom the Senate may choose a Vice President whenever the right of choice shall have devolved upon them.

Section 5.

Sections 1 and 2 shall take effect on the 15th day of October following the ratification of this article.

Section 6.

This article shall be inoperative unless it shall have been ratified as an amendment to the Constitution by the legislatures of three-fourths of the several States within seven years from the date of its submission.

AMENDMENT XXI

Passed by Congress February 20, 1933. Ratified December 5, 1933.

Section 1.

The eighteenth article of amendment to the Constitution of the United States is hereby repealed.

Section 2.

The transportation or importation into any State, Territory, or possession of the United States for delivery or use therein of intoxicating liquors, in violation of the laws thereof, is hereby prohibited.

Section 3.

This article shall be inoperative unless it shall have been ratified as an amendment to the Constitution by conventions in the several States, as provided in the Constitution, within seven years from the date of the submission hereof to the States by the Congress.

AMENDMENT XXII

Passed by Congress March 21, 1947. Ratified February 27, 1951.

Section 1.

No person shall be elected to the office of the President more than twice, and no person who has held the office of President, or acted as President, for more than two years of a term to which some other person was elected President shall be elected to the office of the President more than once. But this Article shall not apply to any person holding the office of President when this Article was proposed by the Congress, and shall not prevent any person who may be holding the office of President, or acting as President, during the term within which this Article becomes operative from holding the office of President or acting as President during the remainder of such term.

Section 2.

This article shall be inoperative unless it shall have been ratified as an amendment to the Constitution by the legislatures of three-fourths of the several States within seven years from the date of its submission to the States by the Congress.

AMENDMENT XXIII

Passed by Congress June 16, 1960. Ratified March 29, 1961.

Section 1.

The District constituting the seat of Government of the United States shall appoint in such manner as the Congress may direct:

A number of electors of President and Vice President equal to the whole number of Senators and Representatives in Congress to which the District would be entitled if it were a State, but in no event more than the least populous State; they shall be in addition to those appointed by the States, but they shall be considered, for the purposes of the election of President and Vice President, to be electors appointed by a State; and they shall meet in the District and perform such duties as provided by the twelfth article of amendment.

Section 2.

The Congress shall have power to enforce this article by appropriate legislation.

AMENDMENT XXIV

Passed by Congress August 27, 1962. Ratified January 23, 1964.

Section 1.

The right of citizens of the United States to vote in any primary or other election for President or Vice President, for electors for President or Vice President, or for Senator or Representative in Congress, shall not be denied or abridged by the United States or any State by reason of failure to pay any poll tax or other tax.

Section 2.
The Congress shall have power to enforce this article by appropriate legislation.

AMENDMENT XXV

Passed by Congress July 6, 1965. Ratified February 10, 1967.

Note: Article II, section 1, of the Constitution was affected by the 25th amendment.

Section 1.
In case of the removal of the President from office or of his death or resignation, the Vice President shall become President.

Section 2.
Whenever there is a vacancy in the office of the Vice President, the President shall nominate a Vice President who shall take office upon confirmation by a majority vote of both Houses of Congress.

Section 3.
Whenever the President transmits to the President pro tempore of the Senate and the Speaker of the House of Representatives his written declaration that he is unable to discharge the powers and duties of his office, and until he transmits to them a written declaration to the contrary, such powers and duties shall be discharged by the Vice President as Acting President.

Section 4.
Whenever the Vice President and a majority of either the principal officers of the executive departments or of such other body as Congress may by law provide, transmit to the President pro tempore of the Senate and the Speaker of the House of Representatives their written declaration that the President is unable to discharge the powers and duties of his office, the Vice President shall immediately assume the powers and duties of the office as Acting President.

Thereafter, when the President transmits to the President pro tempore of the Senate and the Speaker of the House of Representatives his written declaration that no inability exists, he shall resume the powers and duties of his office unless the Vice President and a majority of either the principal officers of the executive department or of such other body as Congress may by law provide, transmit within four days to the President pro tempore of the Senate and the Speaker of the House of Representatives their written declaration that the President is unable to discharge the powers and duties of his office. Thereupon Congress shall decide the issue, assembling within forty-eight hours for that purpose if not in session. If the Congress, within twenty-one days after receipt of the latter written declaration, or, if Congress is not in session, within twenty-one days after Congress is required to assemble, determines by two-thirds vote of both Houses that the President is unable to discharge the powers and duties of his office, the Vice President shall continue to discharge the same as Acting President; otherwise, the President shall resume the powers and duties of his office.

AMENDMENT XXVI

Passed by Congress March 23, 1971. Ratified July 1, 1971.

Note: Amendment 14, section 2, of the Constitution was modified by section 1 of the 26th amendment.

Section 1.
The right of citizens of the United States, who are eighteen years of age or older, to vote shall not be denied or abridged by the United States or by any State on account of age.

Section 2.
The Congress shall have power to enforce this article by appropriate legislation.

AMENDMENT XXVII

Originally proposed Sept. 25, 1789. Ratified May 7, 1992.

No law, varying the compensation for the services of the Senators and Representatives, shall take effect, until an election of Representatives shall have intervened

States' Rights Under the U.S. Constitution

Selective incorporation under the 14th Amendment

The U.S. Constitution has Articles and Amendments that established constitutional rights.

The provisions in the Bill of Rights (i.e., the first ten Amendments to the Constitution) were initially binding upon only the federal government.

In time, most of these provisions became binding upon the states through *selective incorporation* into the *due process clause* of the 14th Amendment (i.e., reverse incorporation).

When a provision is made binding on a state, a state can no longer restrict the rights guaranteed in that provision.

The 1st Amendment guarantees the freedoms of speech, press, religion, and assembly.

The 5th Amendment protects the right to grand jury proceedings in federal criminal cases.

The 6th Amendment guarantees a right to confront witnesses (i.e., Confrontation Clause).

The right to confront witnesses was not *selectively incorporated* into the due process clause of the 14th Amendment and is not binding upon the states.

Therefore, persons involved in state criminal proceedings as a defendant have no federal constitutional right to grand jury proceedings.

Whether an individual has a right to a grand jury becomes a question of state law.

The **10th Amendment**, which is part of the **Bill of Rights**, was ratified on December 15, 1791. It states the Constitution's principle of **federalism** by providing that powers not granted to the **federal government** by the Constitution, nor prohibited to the **States**, are reserved to the States or the people.

Federalism in the United States

Federalism in the United States is the evolving relationship between **state governments** and the **federal government**.

The American government has evolved from a system of dual federalism to associative federalism.

In "Federalist No. 46," James Madison wrote that the states and national government "are in fact but different agents and trustees of the people, constituted with different powers."

Alexander Hamilton, in "Federalist No. 28," suggested that both levels of government would exercise authority to the citizens' benefit: "If their [the peoples'] rights are invaded by either, they can make use of the other as the instrument of redress."[3]

Because the states were preexisting political entities, the U.S. Constitution did not need to define or explain federalism in one section, but it often mentions the rights and responsibilities of state governments and state officials in relation to the federal government.

The federal government has certain *express powers* (also called *enumerated powers*), which are powers spelled out in the Constitution, including the right to levy taxes, declare war, and regulate interstate and foreign commerce.

Also, the *Necessary and Proper Clause* gives the federal government the *implied power* to pass any law "necessary and proper" to execute its express powers.

Enumerated powers of the Federal Government are contained in Article I, Section 8 of the U.S. Constitution.

Other powers—the *reserved powers*—are reserved to the people or the states under the 10th Amendment. The Supreme Court decision significantly expanded the power delegated to the federal government in *McCulloch v. Maryland* (1819) and the 13th, 14th and 15th, Amendments to the Constitution following the **Civil War**.

Law Essentials series

Constitutional Law	Criminal Law and Criminal Procedure
Contracts	Business Associations
Evidence	Conflict of Laws
Real Property	Family Law
Torts	Secured Transactions
Civil Procedure	Trusts and Estates

Visit our Amazon store

Comprehensive Glossary of Legal Terms

Over 2,100 essential legal terms defined and explained. An excellent reference source for law students, practitioners and readers seeking an understanding of legal vocabulary and its application.

Landmark U.S. Supreme Court Cases: Essential Summaries

Learn important constitutional cases that shaped American law. Understand how the evolving needs of society intersect with the U.S. Constitution. Short summaries of seminal Supreme Court cases focused on issues and holdings.

Visit our Amazon store

Frank J. Addivinola, Ph.D., J.D., L.LM., MBA

The lead author and chief editor of this preparation guide is Dr. Frank Addivinola. With his outstanding education, professional training, legal and business experience, and university teaching, Dr. Addivinola lent his expertise to develop this book.

Attorney Frank Addivinola is admitted to practice law in several jurisdictions. He has served as an academic advisor and mentor for students and practitioners.

Dr. Addivinola holds an undergraduate degree from Williams College. He completed his Masters at Harvard University, Masters in Biotechnology at Johns Hopkins University, Masters in Technology Management and MBA at the University of Maryland University College, J.D. and L.LM. from Suffolk University, and Ph.D. in Law and Public Policy from Northeastern University.

During his extensive teaching career, Dr. Addivinola taught university courses in Introduction to Law and developed law coursebooks. He received several awards for community service, research, and presentations.

www.ingramcontent.com/pod-product-compliance
Lightning Source LLC
Chambersburg PA
CBHW081345070526
44578CB00005B/730